WRITERS AND THEIR WORK

ISOBEL ARMSTRONG
Consultant Editor

ROBERT LOUIS STEVENSON

ROBERT LOUIS STEVENSON

David Robb

First published in 2015 by Northcote House Publishers Ltd, Mary Tavy, Tavistock, Devon, PL19 9PY, United Kingdom.
Tel: +44 (0) 1822 810066 Fax: +44 (0) 1822 810034.

British Library Cataloguing-in-Publication Data
A catalogue record for this book is available from the British Library

ISBN 978-0-7463-1101-1 hardcover
ISBN 978-0-7463-0957-5 paperback

Typeset by PDQ Typesetting, Newcastle-under-Lyme
Printed and bound by CPI Group (UK) Ltd, Croydon, CR0 4YY

DEDICATION

To the younger generation
Anna, Fiona, and Tom
and
Ailsa

Contents

Acknowledgements

The present volume is the result, simply, of a prolonged encounter between myself and Stevenson's writings. Consequently, the list of people I must thank for their contribution to its final form is short indeed, consisting essentially of the publisher's reader whose comments were knowledgeable, wise, and encouraging (advice which I was delighted to follow and which enabled me to find the book's proper shape) and my copy-editor. Beyond that immediate support, I owe an immense debt to the many writers who have written, and who continue to write, about Stevenson and his work. During my academic life, critical enthusiasm for Stevenson has become much more widespread than it was when I began, and I have been able to benefit from many recent discussions. Nevertheless, the usual disclaimer that any errors are purely the author's own is particularly true in this case.

It is a pleasure, however, to add two further words of thanks. One is to all those concerned with its planning and production at Northcote House Publishers Ltd, particularly Brian Hulme whose patience and encouragement, over a long period of time, have been extraordinary. The other is to the friend and colleague who first suggested to them my name for a study of Stevenson, Professor Stan Smith. I'm deeply grateful to both and I hope the book is what they envisaged.

Biographical Outline

1850	Robert Louis Stevenson born in Edinburgh (13 November), into a strict religious family. For two previous generations, including Louis's father Thomas, the Stevensons were leading civil engineers, specializing in lighthouses in particular.
1852	Alison Cunningham ('Cummy') taken on as Louis's nurse. She became a formative influence on his imagination, and *A Child's Garden of Verses* was later dedicated to her.
1862–3	Travels with parents to Germany, the Riviera, and Italy.
1867	Enters Edinburgh University, to study engineering (as expected by the family).
1871	Decides to study law instead. Develops close friendship with his cousin Bob Stevenson. His student days are marked by explorations of Edinburgh's seamier side: he enjoys the company of prostitutes and affects a 'bohemian' style of dress and demeanour.
1872	Passes preliminary examinations for the Scottish Bar.
1873	Admits to his father that he is an agnostic, causing a family crisis. His friendship with Sidney Colvin begins. As a result of his ill health during this year, travels south, to Menton in France. This is the first of his attempts to travel out of Scotland in search of somewhere more conducive to his better health.
1874	After several months in Menton, returns to university in Edinburgh. Writes for *Cornhill Magazine*.
1875	Meets W. E. Henley in Edinburgh. Called to the Scottish Bar, but chooses not to begin a legal career.

	Joins his cousin Bob at an artist's colony in the Forest of Fontainebleau. Contributes to the *Academy* and *Vanity Fair*.
1876	Explores the canals of Belgium and northern France in a canoe, a trip which is the basis for *An Inland Voyage*. Meets, and falls in love with, the married American Fanny Osbourne, who has two children.
1877	With Fanny for much of the year, in Paris.
1878	Fanny returns to California where her divorce begins. Stevenson makes his journey on foot in the Cevennes. *An Inland Voyage* and *Edinburgh: Picturesque Notes* published.
1879	Impetuously and despite serious ill-health, Stevenson makes the long, difficult journey, on his own, to California (see *The Amateur Emigrant*). Fanny obtains a divorce in December. *Travels with a Donkey* published.
1880	Almost dies in San Francisco. Marries Fanny in May and they retreat to the Californian mountains (see *The Silverado Squatters*) where Stevenson's health improves for a time. They return to Scotland and are reconciled with Thomas Stevenson. Stevenson's first play *Deacon Brodie* (written with W. E. Henley) published.
1881	The family holiday in Scotland in which Stevenson writes 'Thrawn Janet' and 'The Merry Men' (in Pitlochry) and the first fifteen chapters of *Treasure Island* (in Braemar). This is completed in Davos, Switzerland, and serialized in *Young Folks*, October 1881–January 1882. *Virginibus Puerisque* published.
1882	From Davos, the couple move to Hyères in France. *Familiar Studies of Men and Books* and *New Arabian Nights* published.
1883	*Treasure Island* and *The Silverado Squatters* published – the book publication of *Treasure Island* is his first major success. *The Black Arrow* serialized in *Young Folks* (June–October).
1884	Stevenson and Fanny return to Britain from Hyères and settle in Bournemouth where they will stay until 1887. Stevenson's health continues to cause major concerns. Stevenson and Henley publish

more joint works. Stevenson publishes 'A Humble Remonstrance' (December) in response to Henry James's 'The Art of Fiction' (September).

1885   Thomas Stevenson gives Fanny, as a wedding present, a house in Bournemouth, 'Skerryvore', where Henry James visits them. Stevenson begins *Kidnapped* but lays it aside. He publishes *A Child's Garden of Verses*, *Prince Otto*, *More New Arabian Nights: The Dynamiter* (with Fanny), *Macaire* (with Henley). Has the dream which was the origin of *Jekyll and Hyde*, which he writes at great speed.

1886   *Strange Case of Dr Jekyll and Mr Hyde* published (January): this finally cements his reputation among his contemporaries. *Kidnapped* finished by May and serialized in *Young Folks* (May–July).

1887   Thomas Stevenson dies in May. Stevenson, his mother, Fanny, and Lloyd Osbourne (stepson) depart for America, spending the winter of 1887–8 at Saranac in the Adirondack Mountains, which had become a place of treatment for tubercular patients. Publication of *The Merry Men and Other Tales and Fables*, of *Underwoods*, of *Memoirs and Portraits*, of 'The Misadventures of John Nicholson', and of *A Memoir of Fleeming Jenkin*.

1888   The publishers Scribners commission a book on the South Seas: the party explore there in the chartered yacht *Casco*. Publication of *The Black Arrow*.

1889   Stevenson's mother returns to Scotland. The others continue to explore the South Seas; Stevenson decides to buy an estate in Samoa. *The Master of Ballantrae* is published, as is *The Wrong Box* (with Lloyd).

1890   A further South Sea voyage; the Stevensons realize that Louis's precarious health means that he will have to spend the rest of his life in that part of the world. They settle in Samoa, building the house he names Vailima. Begins writing *David Balfour* [*Catriona*] but abandons it after one chapter. Publication of *In the South Seas* and *Ballads*.

1891   Moves in to the new house. He is given the name 'Tusitala' (writer of tales) by the Samoans. Works on

	The Wrecker (with Lloyd) and on *A Footnote to History*. Writes a little more of *David Balfour*.
1892	Stevenson becomes further involved with local politics. Resumes work on *David Balfour* and completes it in September. It is serialized in *Atlanta* (December 1892–September 1893). Publication of *Across the Plains, A Footnote to History, The Wrecker*.
1893	War in Samoa: Stevenson lends support to side led by Mataafa. Publication of *Island Nights' Entertainments* and *Catriona*.
1894	Publication of *The Ebb-Tide*. Dies suddenly (3 December) of a cerebral haemorrhage.
1896	*Weir of Hermiston* published posthumously. The unfinished *St Ives* begins serialization at the end of the year.

Abbreviations and References

Unless otherwise stated, references in this book to Stevenson's writings are to the Skerryvore Edition of the Works of Robert Louis Stevenson, 30 vols (London: Heinemann, 1924–6). The roman figure after the titles listed below is the volume number. This is also given at first reference to individual titles in the text along with title abbreviation and page number.

BA	*The Black Arrow* VII
BF	'The Beach of Falesá' in *South Sea Tales*, ed. Roslyn Jolly (Oxford: Oxford University Press, 1996)
C.	*Catriona* VI
D.	*The Dynamiter* III
E-T	*The Ebb-Tide* in *South Sea Tales*, ed. Roslyn Jolly (Oxford: Oxford University Press, 1996)
JH	*Strange Case of Dr Jekyll and Mr Hyde*, ed. Roger Luckhurst (Oxford: Oxford University Press, 2006)
JN	'The Misadventures of John Nicholson' XII
K.	*Kidnapped*, ed. Ian Duncan (Oxford: Oxford University Press, 2014)
M.	'Markheim' VII
Maixner	Paul Maixner, *Robert Louis Stevenson: The Critical Heritage* (London, Boston, & Henley: Routledge & Kegan Paul, 1981)
Mehew	*Selected Letters of Robert Louis Stevenson*, ed. Ernest Mehew (New Haven & London: Yale University Press, 2001)
MM	'The Merry Men' VII
O.	'Olalla' VI
PO	*Prince Otto* IV

Poole	*The Master of Ballantrae*, ed. Adrian Poole (London: Penguin Books, 1996)
TF	'The Treasure of Franchard' VII
TI	*Treasure Island*, ed. Peter Hunt (Oxford: Oxford University Press, 2011)
TJ	'Thrawn Janet' VII
WH	*Weir of Hermiston* XIV

1

Introduction: Travels With and Without a Donkey

Between 22 September and 3 October 1878, Stevenson walked through the Cevennes, in the south of France, taking refuge in a solitary holiday soon after the departure of Fanny Osbourne for America. He had fallen in love with the married, but soon to be divorced, American, whom he would eventually marry in May 1880 after a far more arduous and health-threatening journey from Scotland to San Francisco to re-join her. The French walking holiday was his response to her sudden return home at her distant husband's bidding, and was his attempt to deal with the depression which overcame him at their separation. The result was a small book which proved to be his first noticeable success with readers and critics. *Travels with a Donkey in the Cevennes* was written on the basis of the diary he kept on his trip, in December 1878 and January 1879, and was published in June of that year. Under its surface of gracefulness and humour, it covertly expresses his sad longing for the woman with whom he had begun a very intense relationship.

Travels with a Donkey is well worth reading for its own sake, but it can also serve as an introduction to Stevenson because it foreshadows much that emerges in his writing career as a whole. To some extent, this is accidental: the book is short and so was Stevenson's lifetime before the public. Only fifteen years separate the publications of *Travels with a Donkey* and *The Ebb-Tide*. Other similarities seem a little more embedded in Stevenson's writing personality.

The motif of travelling is obvious, of course. Stevenson was one of British literature's great travellers. His adult life saw him constantly re-locating both within and outside Britain, often for reasons of health, and few other writers can match the apparent boldness of his settling in Samoa for the final phase of his life. Our consciousness of the various places Stevenson lived in is a fundamental part of our sense of Stevenson himself: where many great nineteenth-century writers are associated in our minds with individual environments (Dickens with London, George Eliot with the Midlands, the Brontës with Yorkshire, etc.) Stevenson lived in a considerable diversity of places, all of which left their mark on his writing: Edinburgh, an artist's colony in France, the south of England, California, New York State, the South Seas. And that association, in our minds, of Stevenson and place is reflected in the degree to which place is integral to his stories. So it seems fitting that this first popular publication (the immediately preceding travel book, *An Inland Voyage*, made, and still makes, a lesser impression) is devoted to the author's encounter with a particular region. Not that the scenery is his primary concern. He is interested in the people he meets, and in his own interaction with them. The landscape of the Cevennes is the backdrop to his adventures, and provides the physical challenge which stimulates his efforts.

Equally, travelling would become one of his regular story-elements, as many of his best-known works testify: the journeys of Jim Hawkins and David Balfour (in both of the books in which he appears) simply confirm the centrality of journeying in the imaginative worlds Stevenson offers. Nor is it stretching the image too far, I think, to see Stevenson's fictional output as marking a notably long and surprisingly varied journey, from *New Arabian Nights* to *The Ebb-Tide*, despite the short time between them. If readers nowadays base their sense of Stevenson solely on a tiny number of well-known tales, such as *Jekyll and Hyde* and *Treasure Island*, which exist as much in the general culture as they do in actual reading-experience, then an examination of more of his writing, in all its variety, is likely to produce some surprise.

'Surprise' is one of the essential qualities of Stevenson's writing – the point is Alistair Fowler's in a key essay.[1] Stevenson's tales deal less in the tensions of suspense than in the surprises of unexpected turns of events. Just as Stevenson in the Cevennes did not know what each day would bring, so the reader journeys with him through his tales, embarking on each new chapter as on a new and unknown stretch of country. His characters encounter life, not as a mystery to be solved but as a landscape to be explored, grappled with and survived. Stevenson's stories confront their protagonists with a series of challenges, often of the most unexpected kind: this, perhaps, is what most strongly links his earliest and later fictions. And it is this which forms the basis of his version of romance: everyday normalities (whether those of the streets of nineteenth-century London, or of a broken-down old house not far from the Firth of Forth, an obscure country inn in a quiet part of England, a family castle in the land of Walter Scott, the drawing-rooms of respectable London or Edinburgh, or the unrespectable corners of Tahiti) produce utterly unpredictable developments which challenge and reveal the essential quality of his protagonists.

In the traversal of the Cevennes, the challenging surprises arise not so much from the terrain or the peasantry, but from Modestine, the donkey Stevenson bought to transport his gear. Predictably, much that is entertaining in the book arises from this creature's behaviour, and Stevenson's response to it. Modestine rapidly becomes a character in the book, and so turns Stevenson himself, from being an observer and reporter, into a character also. Indeed, *Travels with a Donkey* is the first of Stevenson's many tales of duality – of the pairing of contrasted characters, and of the drama of the tussle for dominance between them. So it is one of the many Stevensonian surprises that from Stevenson and Modestine there will eventually emerge Jim and Silver, David and Alan, the two Duries and (yes) Jekyll and Hyde. With Stevenson and Modestine locked in their comic battles, the Cevennes rapidly becomes the setting of a tale: what starts out as a description and a memoir – that is, a travel book – develops into a story, of Stevenson and his donkey. The telling of stories, however, is Stevenson's instinctive way of bringing a place to life. Place and incident exist cheek by jowl in his universe. In his essay 'A Gossip on Romance', he explains the stimulus a place will often give to his imagination. Stories need to be told, he finds, to bring out the uniqueness of a location: 'Some places speak distinctly. Certain dank gardens cry aloud for a murder; certain old houses demand to be haunted; certain coasts are set apart for shipwreck.... The old Hawes Inn at the Queen's Ferry makes a similar call upon my fancy.'[2] The book is

3

not an exact transcription of his Cevennes diary: it edges, rather, towards fiction. We don't doubt the reality of the journey, or the reliability of the accounts of its episodes, yet the sense of artifice is unavoidable, and welcome. Thus, the graceful expression, the wit, the sense that a book is uniquely his, contribute as always to Stevenson's appeal. Few readers nowadays would see themselves as connoisseurs of 'style', but the fact remains that Stevenson's prose is part of his pleasure. And the zest with which he tackles his journey becomes one with the zest with which he writes about it. Entertainment is derived from the petty struggles and difficulties he encounters. His Cevennes journey, after all, was a project both manly and aesthetic, a matter of hearty physical challenge and of the sensitive appreciation of a place and its people. Much of his future appeal is here in embryo.

In the Cevennes, Stevenson was trying to get away from his disappointment over Fanny, but he was also consciously aiming to produce another book. It was not to be the sort of standardized travel book, however, envisaged by the landlady encountered at Bouchet, despite Stevenson's friendly agreement:

> I was tightly cross-examined about my journey; and the lady understood in a moment, and sketched out what I should put into my book when I got home. 'Whether people harvest or not in such or such a place; if there were forests; studies of manners; what, for example, I and the master of the house say to you; the beauties of Nature, and all that.'
> 'It is just that,' said I.[3]

Important as the sense of place may be in Stevenson's work, physical description is always subsidiary to a human drama occurring there; as his discussion in 'A Gossip on Romance' shows, a place is not merely a location, but a site where stories occur. In an account of a journey, Stevenson himself is inevitably his own main character. Of course, the true story he was living – the drama of his relationship with Fanny and the pain of their separation – could not be told in this public way, so the comic, but heartfelt, tale of his dealings with Modestine takes its place. But this is a reminder of how much natural drama, and indeed romance, lies in the story of Stevenson's own life – so much so that an interest in the man himself seems at times to be outlasting the present-day public's interest in his writings. Individual editions of even his best, and best-known, works seldom survive in print for long, and where once 'complete editions' of his writings proliferated, it now seems to be difficult to create a modern scholarly complete edition, whereas the now far less widely read Scott is granted the (admittedly, deserved) honour of just such an edition. In contrast, biographies of Stevenson still seem to arrive at regular intervals. Like Scott's, Stevenson's critical reputation has fluctuated wildly in the years since his death but where Scott now enjoys (whatever the general reader may think) a fairly settled critical regard, thanks to the obvious importance of his intervention in the history of the novel, Stevenson enjoys no similar historical grounding. So far as Stevenson's place in the development of fiction is concerned, he has to be thought of in the later nineteenth century's squabbles about realism and romance. He is surely read now much more widely than Scott, but there is less stability in the view of the academy towards him. Those who make particularly strong claims for him, like Alan Sandison and Frank McLynn, still have to do so with an air of challenge, of boldness.[4] Yet the time of agreeing with David Daiches, that there was a constant immaturity about his writing which was only being shrugged off when he suddenly died, seems past. Stevenson can once again arouse critical enthusiasm, and younger critics like Robert Crawford are willing to take, and welcome, him on his own terms.[5] I hope that the present book does the same, with something of the same openness that Stevenson and his characters showed on their travels.

What follows is a series of discussions of individual fictions. It assumes that the reader is familiar with Stevenson's own story, or has access to one or other of the various recent accounts of his life. Brief biographical reminders serve only to provide introductions to each of the three phases which might be perceived in his writing career – not that one need insist too strongly on those divisions. It has not been possible to discuss in equal detail every piece of Stevenson's fiction: the works discussed are, I think, the crucial ones, along with one or two lesser known examples which reflect some personal preference and which further underline the variety to be found in

Stevenson's astonishing body of writing. I have resisted trying to impose too simple a pattern on the picture of his career. The sequence from *New Arabian Nights* to *The Ebb-Tide* clearly shows great change and while one is constantly tempted to think of the former as 'youthful' and the latter as 'mature', I do not feel that there is a simple line of development which can be easily defined. To help the reader appreciate the surprises of Stevenson's inspiration, I have sequenced the discussions in terms of the order of writing rather than the order of publication. It may heighten the delight of finding what is round the next corner.

2

'A brilliant and romantic grace'

W. E. Henley so describes Stevenson in his sonnet 'Apparition', from his sonnet sequence 'In Hospital' (published 1888). They had met in 1875, when Leslie Stephen brought Stevenson to visit Henley in hospital in Edinburgh. That other literary mentor, Sidney Colvin, introduced to Stevenson in 1873, had been equally fascinated with the young Scot. These were the years when influential men of letters were first realizing that in Stevenson they had found the kind of writer they particularly approved of, and that he and his work were to be nurtured.

Stevenson first began to make an impression on the wider reading public with the important products of 1878–9, *Travels with a Donkey* and *New Arabian Nights*. Thereafter, in the middle of the five-year period which culminated in the writing of *Prince Otto* and *The Black Arrow*, came the work which first caused him to be universally perceived as an important and popular writer, *Treasure Island*. This early period in his career produced, however, not only the story which many still regard as their favourite Stevenson novel of all, but a diverse and fascinating clutch of works which should be better known and more widely enjoyed.

The period 1878–83 was dominated, in personal terms, with the dramas and intensities of his developing relationship with Fanny Osbourne. He had first met her in France in 1876, had come to love her in the succeeding two years, and was desolate when she suddenly returned to California. Stevenson made his quixotic and life-threatening journey in pursuit of her in 1879 and they were married in 1880. They returned to Britain, experiencing the dreich but astonishingly productive family holiday in Pitlochry and Braemar in 1881, where Stevenson wrote 'The Merry Men', 'Thrawn Janet' and most of *Treasure*

Island. Looking for a permanent home away from the Scottish climate, the married couple first tried France, then settled in Bournemouth, Stevenson's health being the ever more urgent consideration.

NEW ARABIAN NIGHTS (WRITTEN 1878)

The stories eventually collected and published in 1882 as a volume entitled *New Arabian Nights* were among Stevenson's very first works of prose fiction. They had been preceded in 1877 by his earliest efforts of all, including the short stories 'A Lodging for the Night', 'The Sire de Maletroit's Door' and 'Will o' the Mill'. From the start, then, Stevenson was producing work which is still very much worth reading today. 'Will o' the Mill' is perhaps the most arresting of the three, though in some ways the least typical of the Stevenson who would finally emerge. It is a parable which seems to advocate that life should be lived as an unambitious, contented, solitary, and inward-looking experi- ence, with no curiosity about what can be found over the horizon – not at all what one associates with Stevenson. What is certainly his, however, is the confidence to be felt in its pace and its writing, and in the memorability of the visionary – indeed, allegorical – scene of Will's encounter with Death. Because part of Stevenson's appeal for many readers of an earlier generation was the feeling that he can teach us about life, this quietistic vision can seem puzzling – but then, Stevenson is a writer who offers more variety than is often realized.

New Arabian Nights, on the other hand, has always struck readers as quintessential Stevenson, both in its delights and its problems, and despite its tone of irresponsible playfulness seeming far from that of some of the great books to come. William Archer is occasionally quoted as writing that Stevenson 'never wrote anything more consummate in their kind than the *New Arabian Nights*; yet one is glad to think that these exercises in blood-curdling humour came at the beginning of his career'.[1] Archer's sense that they are both excellent but also limited has always cross-hatched discussion of them. Even George Saints- bury's original laudatory review in the *Pall Mall Gazette* is shot through with a consciousness of 'faults' in the stories, and an uneasy awareness that there will be 'some good people to whom the book will probably be a simple mystification'.[2] Among critics of our own time, the tales can arouse the extremes of enthusiasm (Alan Sandison) or discomfort (Robert Kiely). To the first modern biographer of Stevenson, J. C. Furnas, the work is 'that spring-heel'd freak', a somewhat dismissive acknowledgement of its strange energy.[3] And dismissal, too, is the implication of the swiftly passing references of more recent biographers (Jenni Calder, Claire Harman) who scarcely linger in their eagerness to get to their author's less puzzling, and still popular, writings.

Even amongst commentators who respond warmly, or at least thoughtfully, to the stories in the collection, there is little consensus about their nature beneath the elegant and self-consciously stylish surface. For Edwin Eigner, they are 'works of almost unalloyed comedy'.[4] J. R. Hammond sees them as a still-developing author's exercise in clarity and economy of style.[5] Alan Sandison, in an extensive and elaborate discussion, argues that they are a masterpiece of subversion, an embodiment of Stevenson's belief in Art as a game, and an expression of a lightly ironic attitude towards everything – Art included.[6] The unsympathetic Kiely, as already noted, believes they attempt satire and fail, by and large. That there are so many different ways of responding to them goes some way to illustrating their attractive peculiarity.

These stories present difficulties when one tries to see them as more weighty than they are. Sandison's instinct that they are the products of a belief in Art as a game is surely correct, although he erects a lengthy argument of immense sophistica-tion on that premise. Those critics who deal with the collection only briefly, on the other hand, share Sandison's way of responding to it while assuming that 'game' implies 'trivia'. Whichever way one leans, one has to see Stevenson here as concerned above all with story-telling – with the pleasures of telling, and of reading, tales. He is performing as a writer, and we are invited to enjoy the performance. The tales' surprises are their essence.

The reader's somewhat startled experience begins even before the narrative proper. The contents page indicates that the collection falls into two main parts, entitled 'The Suicide Club' and 'The Rajah's Diamond'. In turn, these are further subdivided (it would appear) into (respectively) three and four 'stories' or 'adventures'. We are thus promised tales which are both individualized and linked, a Chinese box of narratives. However, on the opening page of the first story, we have to finally assimilate those three utterly different, indeed apparently incompatible, titles, one below the other: 'New Arabian Nights'; 'The Suicide Club'; 'Story of the Young Man with the Cream Tarts'. This excess of helpfulness instantly carries us beyond confusion, to helpless spectatorship: how are these three daft titles going to be reconciled? As we begin to read, we cling to the two somewhat stagey and improbably-named characters to whom we are introduced, Prince Florizel of Bohemia and his equerry Colonel Geraldine. These two provide, as it turns out, the fitful strand of continuity throughout the collection, but their appearances are marked by surprise and unexpectedness, rather than being the means of structural continuity and strength. As a result, the author strikes us forcefully as not so much an observer (as it were) of an imagined reality, but its extremely wilful creator.

Critics have sometimes complained about that wilfulness in Stevenson's cheerful destruction of all illusion with his airy dismissal of Prince Florizel, and of his 'Arabian Author', in the final paragraph of 'The Rajah's Diamond', where he compounds the demonstration of his own authorial arbitrariness by suddenly consigning his Highness to the counter of a cigar shop in central London. If this outraged W. H. Pollock in 1882 (Maixner 110), one might at least point out that the guying of the reader, and the fore fronting of the writer, had actually begun at the very outset, with the ostentatious juxtaposition of the three titles. If the original Arabian Nights Entertainments is as much about the power and process of story-telling as it is about the stories themselves – we participate in Scheherazade's artfulness as much as we subject ourselves to it – then the same is true here. The tales are told both for their own sake and for the sake of revealing how a tale-teller can tell tales. Wilful arbitrariness is the name of the game.

That arbitrariness, and the spirit of mocking gaiety with which it is associated in these tales, is not merely embodied in the flow of Stevenson's invention (whether in the episodes within each tale, or even in that initial trio of titles), nor just in the sprightly energy of the writing. It is a condition of the world he depicts. Florizel and Geraldine are *flâneurs*, intent on deriving entertainment from their chance encounters in the crowded London streets, and the fortuitous meeting with the young man of the cream tarts is merely one of their least predictable. He, in turn, flamboyantly ridding himself of the last of his wealth (apart from the £40 entrance fee for the Suicide Club), is mocking himself, his 'customers' and the whole conduct of responsible society. Arbitrariness is carried over, too, into the central idea of this first tale, that of the 'game' of cards which the club members play to choose killer and victim. The world of *New Arabian Nights* is one in which the unexpected is a fundamental condition, and while it could be argued that the unexpected is a requirement of any piece of effective tale-telling (and it continues to be a natural and key element in all Stevenson's later fictions) it is here deployed with a flamboyance which places *New Arabian Nights* in a world of its own. So the bizarre cheerfulness of the encounter with the young man and his tarts leads, suddenly, to the darkness of the Suicide Club itself. The comical sexual immaturity of the young American in Paris leads to the corpse of Geraldine's brother in his bed. Brackenbury Rich's purposeless encounter with the London scene – he asks a cabman to drive him 'where you please' – takes him to the mysterious party which turns out to be, in turn, a device to select two hardy seconds for Prince Florizel in his duel with the President of the Suicide Club. Harry Hartley's simple errand, in 'The Rajah's Diamond', to deliver a hatbox to a particular London address, turns into a tale of comic fisticuffs, grand theft, and the erratic journey of a priceless diamond. (Wilkie Collins's *The Moonstone* had been published only ten years previously.)

As in the Arabian Nights original, the continuities of character merely serve to underline the arbitrariness of the individual tales: Florizel appears with the suddenness of a genie and with a genie's capability to resolve the apparently unresolvable difficulties in which events have placed the protagonist of the moment. With each successive sighting of the prince, the reader feels, momentarily, more 'in the know' than the young men thrashing about in the mysteries in which they are caught, but we are as much the outsiders in Stevenson's game as the characters themselves. That sense that the author is always one step ahead of everyone, characters and readers alike, is fundamental to the work.

'THE MERRY MEN' (WRITTEN 1881)

'The Merry Men', written in Pitlochry, along with 'Thrawn Janet' and 'The Body Snatcher', presents the modern reader with none of the puzzlement and unease of Stevenson's 'Arabian' tales. We feel that we know where we are with it: Scottish history and landscape, the Calvinist conscience, physical excitement and tragedy, and a Scott-inspired clash of ancient and modern outlooks assure us that *Kidnapped, Catriona, The Master of Ballantrae* and *Weir of Hermiston* are already distantly on the horizon. We feel assured, too, that Stevenson is certain of the effects he is after. Furthermore, the tale has a richness and complexity, a range of themes and interests, which stimulate different biographers and commentators to different emphases in their summaries of what it is about. While perhaps not flawless, it is now regarded as one of Stevenson's early undoubted successes.

It combines two dimensions over which the maturing Stevenson would prove a master: the psychological and moral struggle between good and evil, and the fusion of a human story with regional (indeed, topographical) specificity. The setting on a tiny Scottish west coast outpost, far from any modern city and confronting the full might of the sea, seems entirely appropriate for this tale of superstition, twisted morality, a stricken conscience, and madness, partly thanks to the elemental power and grandeur of the isolated location and thanks, also, to the weave of local history and tradition upon which Stevenson confidently bases his story. The Stevenson family, creators of lighthouses, were fully familiar with the dark traditions of isolated coastal communities, and Louis's own narrative of his family's engineering exploits, *Records of a Family of Engineers*, contains an account of his father's youthful encounter in the Pentland Firth with a hamlet full of wreckers, who patiently and callously awaited the destruction (which, in the event, never happened) of the lighthouse inspection vessel.[7] The twisted and (to outsiders) almost unfathomable morality of the wrecker's state of mind clearly reinforced Stevenson's deep instinct for the moral complexity of the human species and for the moral contradictions to be found in the world as a whole. (Near the end of the story, the narrator talks of the Merry Men – the gigantic roaring breakers occasioned by the deadly submerged rocks off the coast – as 'part of the world's evil and the tragic side of life'. (VII, MM 61)) Stevenson's central character, however, is entirely lacking in the calm moral numbness of the traditional wrecker: Gordon Darnaway is a Calvinist in the old Cameronian mould, with a lively sense of hell and punishment, and of the world as an arena for the great battle between Good and Evil, God and the Devil. He persuades himself that the destructive bounty of the sea, with which (with surreal effect) he adorns his isolated cottage, can be welcomed and accepted as the will of a cruel god.

The story is set in the latter decades of the eighteenth century, when the rationalism of the Scottish Enlightenment (the narrator's university mentor is the prominent Enlightenment historian, Principal William Robertson) co-existed with the sturdy traditions of a less rationalist outlook, manifested both in the traditions of an earlier phase of Scottish Christianity and also in the still strong folklore beliefs of Scottish country folk. Darnaway is steeped in both, with the result that, unlike (say) James Hogg's youthful justified sinner, he seems less fearful of the horrors of eternal damnation than he is of the possibility of being claimed, in this life, by some punitively terrifying devil. He and his servant Rorie believe that land and sea both are haunted by bogles – in effect, devils who threaten both mind and body. Stevenson carefully explores Darnaway's state of mind, in preparation for the tragic climax when, by now entirely mad, he flees to his death from the negro survivor of a shipwreck, believing him to be either (or both) the ghost of an earlier shipwrecked seaman he had murdered or the devil himself, in the form (characteristic of Scottish folklore) of a black man. Darnaway's inner state, sketched in word and deed, is one of the triumphs of the tale: he does not simply slip from good to evil, but rather comes to revel in wickedness, both that of the world and that of his own heart. He is intoxicated by the destructive roar of the sea, crowned by the infernal noise of the Merry Men:

'See to them!' he continued, dragging me to the edge of the abyss from whence arose that deafening clamour and those clouds of spray; 'see to them dancin', man! Is that no wicked?'

He pronounced the word with gusto, and I thought it suited the scene. (MM 46)

Later, Darnaway is even more startlingly open about his identification with the evil and destructiveness of the world, and describes how he is at one with the awfulness of the storm even as it destroys ships and men:

'You are a religious man,' I replied, 'and this is sin.'

'Ou,' he returned, 'if it wasna sin, I dinna ken that I would care for't. Ye see, man, it's defiance. There's a sair spang o' the auld sin o' the warld in yon sea; it's an unchristian business at the best o't; an' whiles when it gets up, an' the wind skreighs...an' thae Merry Men, the daft callants, blawin' and lauchin', and puir souls in the deid thraws warstlin' the leelang nicht wi' their bit ships – weel, it comes ower me like a glamour. I'm a deil, I ken't. But I think naething o' the puir sailor lads; I'm wi' the sea, I'm just like ane o' her ain Merry Men.' (MM 50)

'The Merry Men' is one of Stevenson's earlier treatments of the mystery and complexity of evil and Darnaway prefigures such characters as Edward Hyde, James Durie, and (from just a little later in the summer of 1881) Long John Silver.

The story is usually discussed, consequently, as evidence of the growing presence of his Calvinist inheritance in Stevenson's creative imagination, especially when it is remembered that 'Thrawn Janet' was written during the same summer. Darnaway, solidly sketched, is a thorough old-style Scottish Calvinist, with his polarized vision of the moral universe, his insistence that God's will cannot be interfered with, his positive delight in the destruction and damnation of the sea's victims, and his insistence that the dead cannot be prayed for (in his eyes, a sign of papistry). Furthermore, Stevenson seems to strive to give the whole story a certain religious-cum-moral dimension, over and above the religious consciousness of his eighteenth-century characters. The scene is on a near-island called Aros, which we are told means The House of God, while the wrecked ship which had occasioned the crime which haunts Darnaway was the *Christ-Anna*, the Follower of Christ. And the Spanish treasure ship which intrigues the young narrator and which lures a team

of Spanish treasure-hunters to their deaths was the *Espirito Santo*
– the Holy Spirit. The striking story, focused upon the small
handful of characters, takes on broader overtones as Stevenson
hints at the eternal conflict of values (between worldliness and
holiness) within which they struggle, and at the challenge of the
world's evil, treacherous, and immovable in both the human
heart and in God's Creation as a whole. In a letter to Colvin, a
few years later, he admitted that he had been in the habit of
brooding 'on the evil in the world and man' (Maixner 250) and
that this had been particularly manifest in the products of his
summer of 1881.

Yet 'The Merry Men' is far from being a simple Christian
morality: rather, it celebrates the awfulness of the sea at a more
powerfully primitive level still. That the sea is, in a way, the
essential heart of this story is confirmed by Stevenson's own
description of it (in the same letter to Colvin) as 'a fantasia or
vision of the sea'. We have no need, however, of this
confirmation: alongside the tale of Darnaway's twisted life and
startling end, the story fills our awareness with a sense of the
sea, so extensively, minutely, and lovingly described by
Stevenson. Supremely successful is the evocation of the sea at
its most powerful, awesome, and memorable – an evocation so
thorough and complete that Stevenson even creates a scene *in* it,
under the waves. Given the family business of lighthouse-
building, it is perhaps not to be wondered at that the sea is seen
as an alien element, from which human beings require all the
safety precautions which can be devised. It is associated with
death, and both Darnaway and his nephew Charlie experience at
close quarters its character as a domain of the dead. We are half-
led to agree with Darnaway's near-insane gasp, 'the horror – the
horror o' the sea!' (MM 18), especially while we read the
magnificently harrowing description of the slow entrapment
and wreck of the Spanish schooner.

The story's success, in all likelihood, is not solely the result of
Stevenson's switch to the Scottish world which would continue
to prove so fruitful for him. At least one other major difference
between 'The Merry Men' and several others of his early fictions
is the fact that he is here creating and telling the story through
the eyes, mind, and speech of one of the characters. Where in
the Arabian tales, and in the subsequent *Prince Otto*, narration is

omniscient, so that the invention is consequently free to be as whimsical and personal as Stevenson liked, he is here working within a different set of constraints – of history and place, of mental outlook, of voice. Not that Charlie, his narrator, is given to any marked individuality of expression. But with this setting and material, Stevenson was freed at a stroke from the impulse to invent a romantic, Ruritanian, stylishly 'aesthetic' world. The consciousness of eighteenth-century Scottish West Highlanders, formed from evangelical Calvinism and ancient folk-beliefs and confronting daily something as elemental as the ocean's fury, required no authorial transformations. Reality, if appropriately selected, can be romantic enough.

'THRAWN JANET' (WRITTEN 1881)

'Thrawn Janet', another achievement of that wet summer, has a prominent place in current estimates of Stevenson's work. It appeals to Scottish critics particularly, as it is unusual in being written almost completely in Scots prose, something which by and large has not been followed up by many other writers. It is one of a small handful of frequently anthologized nineteenth-century short stories (Scott's 'Wandering Willie's Tale' and Stevenson's own 'Tale of Tod Lapraik' are probably the other best known examples) which do the same. In most of his other works, Stevenson follows Scott's practice and confines Scots to dialogue, retaining English for the narrative itself. Stevenson's love of Scots, nevertheless, is clear from the many examples in his writing, a love which is further confirmed by his poetry and by statements in his non-fictional prose. Thus, his 1887 poetry collection *Underwoods* contains a substantial number of poems in Scots, as well as an appendix of several paragraphs discussing his latitudinarian attitude towards preciseness in differentiating between different dialects of Scots, and offering his own amateurishly practical guide to the pronunciation of the Scots poems in the book. Also, the appendix ends with a coronach (funeral song) contemplating the dying out of Scots in everyday use:

> The day draws near when this illustrious and malleable tongue shall be quite forgotten; and Burns's Ayrshire, and Dr. Macdonald's

Aberdeen-awa', and Scott's brave, metropolitan utterance will be all equally the ghosts of speech. Till then I would love to have my hour as a native Maker, and be read by my own countryfolk in our own dying language: an ambition surely rather of the heart than of the head, so restricted as it is in prospect of endurance, so parochial in bounds of space.[8]

Alongside this, we can place an assertion in a letter to Colvin (April 1893) in a defence of *Catriona*, Chapter 15 of which is largely made up of 'The Tale of Tod Lapraik': '"Tod Lapraik" is a piece of living Scots: If I had never writ anything but that and "Thrawn Janet", still I'd have been a writer.'[9] An initial glance at 'Thrawn Janet', therefore, might suggest that it is merely an exercise in linguistic nostalgia, while a first reading confirms its aim to make our flesh creep. A fresh, confident, bookish young minister protects Janet M'Clour, recommended to him as a housekeeper by the local laird, from the physical persecution of a mob of women who believe her to be a witch – Mr Soulis (and presumably the laird) disapproves of all such superstitions. Janet is an outcast presence in the community, thanks to a decades-old sexual misdemeanour and to her general lack of conformity to the expectations of the clachan (hamlet). The day after her rough handling, she appears with her head perma-nently on one side, her face contorted, and with an inability to speak properly. Soulis realizes that she has had a stroke but to the rest of the villagers she is merely even more uncanny than before. Her appearance resembles that of a hanged corpse, and they begin to think of her as dead but animated by the devil. While out walking during a spell of particularly oppressive, heavy summer weather, Soulis encounters a black man in an old, disused graveyard. (And Stevenson provides a footnote pointing to the old Scottish superstition that the devil some-times appears as a black man.) This unexpected apparition runs off, not to be caught, and seems to disappear inside the manse itself. When Soulis gets home, however, Janet denies that any such person had entered the house. As night falls, Soulis is gradually overcome with a new superstitious belief that the clachan is indeed correct about Janet. He comes round to the idea that there is a connection between Janet and the black man, at which point an unexpected noise in Janet's room next door prompts him to investigate: he finds her hanged, suspended from a solitary nail by means of a single thread of darning wool. Shocked (as well he might be), he retreats downstairs, until he hears footsteps in Janet's room, followed by her locked door opening and her presence sensed at the top of the stair. Eventually forced to confront the walking corpse, he is saved only by his godly challenge to the being as she/it draws ever nearer: the Lord's name causes the corpse to burst into flames and collapse to the ground in a heap of ashes. Needless to say, Soulis is never the same man again. A classic Victorian ghost story, then, with a very Scottish accent?

Stevenson is here working at the interface between folk superstition and Enlightenment rationality — an interface that had been a social and cultural reality in Scotland for more than a century by the time he wrote the story. It had provided his great predecessors Burns, Scott, and Hogg with much of their best material, each of them living in at least two very different Scottish worlds. The riches of rural Scottish folk-song, folk-tale, and folk-belief formed, for each of them, a counterpoint to, and immense enlargement of, the world revealed by the rationality of the Scottish Enlightenment. Nor was this interaction confined to Scott's lifetime, the main moment of Romanticism in Scotland: Victorian writers such as George MacDonald and Margaret Oliphant continued to challenge the materialist view of the world with their own sense of a reality crucially other than, and greater than, that in which we feel daily confined. Stevenson's instinct for a romance vision is an example of a later nineteenth-century version of the same dualism, and it is no surprise that this instinct should have stimulated from him occasional fictions which hark back to the writings of his Scottish predecessors.

But whereas Burns and Hogg incorporated the folk vision into their work with sympathetic enthusiasm, the result of their appreciation of the country life which had formed them, and whereas Scott had responded to Scottish balladry with the commitment of a Romantic ballad-collector, Stevenson's relationship with the folk tradition was subtly different. Very much the product of Victorian Edinburgh, his contact with the folk tradition had been the stories of his nurse Alison Cunningham and while he clearly responded, both as a child and as a man, to the imaginative richness of this material, he also associated it with the night-time terrors which had been such a feature of his childhood. The folk tradition, though powerfully presented to him by 'Cummy', had been less of an integral part of his boyhood world than it had been for Burns and Hogg; rather, it had been somewhat at odds with the middle-class environment which was moulding him, and had introduced into it a sense of the otherworldly as something intrusive, disquieting, and destructive. Stevenson has none of the easy familiarity with the supernatural which we find in other Scottish nineteenth-century authors and he would never respond to the devil (who first appears in his fiction in this product of the summer of 1881), with Burns's companionable familiarity or with Hogg's witty appreciation of his stylish, if demonic, ingenuity. Rather, Stevenson's devil-figures are always hatefully malevolent, and play tragically destructive roles in the moral patterns of his stories.

In 'Thrawn Janet', the point of the story is a double one. At one level, the tale enacts the literalness with which the devil must have appeared in Cummy's stories: it is a recreation of the folk-belief in straightforward, real supernatural evil. And much of its force derives from this: what everyone remembers most vividly is the delicious realism of Soulis listening to the corpse's approach from the bedroom, his awareness of its downward look over the stair-rail (and his inability to look upwards to return that look), the slow audible descent of the thing, and its eventual appearance to the minister's appalled gaze. This is a ghost (or whatever) which we can fully imagine; for us, as for Soulis, this devil is (for the moment) real.

At another level, however, Janet's walking corpse is an embodiment of the primitively superstitious frame of mind to which Soulis reverts: she is filled with the devil, as is the world as seen by the clachan. This is an encounter, and a belief, which destroys the good man who acts so charitably towards Janet when she is attacked. The aged Soulis is first presented to us as 'a severe, bleak-faced old man, dreadful to his hearers' who combines 'iron composure' with an eye 'wild, scared, and uncertain', whose mind is dominated by 'the terrors of eternity', and whose ministry essentially consists of scaring the wits out of everyone he encounters (VII, TJ 121). He is a caricature of a backwoods preacher in the Covenanting tradition, the kind of pastor satirized so frequently by Burns, and so disliked by Scott (despite his attempts at historical understanding). It is likely, too, that Soulis conforms to what many of Stevenson's first readers will have thought of as a type of traditional Scottish clergyman. Only twenty years earlier, for example, the second volume of Buckle's *History of Civilisation in England* had appeared, in which he had described Scots in the eighteenth and even the nineteenth centuries as still dominated by 'a few noisy and ignorant preachers, to whom it allows a license, and yields a submission' with the result (said Buckle) that they are a people who 'upon all religious subjects, display a littleness of mind, an illiberality of sentiment, a heat of temper, and a love of persecuting others, which shows that the Protestantism of which they boast has done them no good'. To Buckle, and doubtless to many other English Victorians, the Scots were still largely enslaved by religious prejudices 'which have turned the very name of the Scotch Kirk into a by-word and a reproach among educated men'.[10] The elderly Soulis would appear to be one of those noisy and ignorant preachers: when he first started out, however, he had been a modest embodiment of Enlightenment values. Which was why his first parishioners had regarded him as 'a self-deceiver' 'wi' nae leevin' experience in religion', someone under whom 'the parish...was like to be sae ill-supplied' (TJ 122–3). But if the longevity of his ministry is any guide, it would seem that, however disconcerting, his latter-day wild-eyed version of pastoral care was now essentially satisfactory to his flock. Stevenson is playing up the image of Scots as steeped in the gloomiest of religions.

Stevenson employs a near-Dickensian choice of names, Murdoch Soulis, for his grim protagonist, and the pervasive bleakness (with a hint of national caricature) is gently underlined by the place-name details he provides: Soulis's parish is 'the moorland parish of Balweary, in the vale of Dule'. ('Dule' is a Scots word meaning grief or distress.) His dwelling is 'the small and lonely manse under the Hanging Shaw' (a 'shaw' is a small wood) (TJ 121). Soulis's existence is isolated and lonely, and his demeanour and personality clearly repel all who encounter him. It is difficult to read the tale as one in which a cocky young intellectual is chastened and transformed into a sadder and a wiser man; rather it is the story of a life destroyed. And the destruction does not consist merely in his being bludgeoned into a wildly superstitious set of beliefs, abandoning the humane charity which he had brought to Balweary; it involves the adoption of a creed which runs counter to human companionship and to any human peace of mind. He embodies a vision of religious terror which blights the community, but which is nevertheless accepted by it.

'Thrawn', in one of its two major usages, means 'wilfully and persistently stubborn': 'Thrawn Janet' is stubborn Janet – and so she is, in the most obvious sense of she's-dead-but-she-won't-lie-down. The other meaning of the word applies equally: 'thrawn' is twisted, distorted, and is frequently applied to the fatal twisting of a neck, in the slaying of a chicken, or of a condemned person. Whether or not she was kept in apparent life by the devil, Janet embodied the persistence of what the community chose to regard as evil, and even decades later it would appear (assuming that any of this ever happened at all) that her evil reality continues to twist and distort the life of the minister. But dominant in the tale is the persistence of the community's ideology, which demonizes human frailty and scapegoats those who do not conform to its ways. Both Janet and Soulis are the community's victims – Soulis is a full-blown fisher-king with a never-healing wound, but whose sacrifice of his enlightened beliefs and of his sanity ends the oppressive drought which had afflicted the area in the days before his fateful encounter. His subsequent crazed ferocity appears to be the necessary condition for community stability. What also persists, however, are the consequences of the memorable encounter the tale recounts – consequences in the lives of both the minister and his community, bleak and joyless in both cases. However wicked Janet may have been, she lives on in the way of life subsequently on offer in Balweary: whatever she was or represented lives on and her apparent defeat has brought no earthly paradise to the godly. She is 'thrawn' indeed.

'Thrawn Janet' is a tale told by 'one of the older folk' of the clachan, only a couple of introductory paragraphs being given to an English-speaking narrator. Stevenson, like Hogg before him, takes advantage of the inherent factual unreliability of oral tradition to have his narrative cake and eat it as well: we as readers simultaneously 'believe' and don't believe in the wildly impossible tale which unfolds. But whereas in Hogg's *Justified*

Sinner nobody in the novel's 'present' knows what to believe about Wringhim's life and personality, in 'Thrawn Janet' the representative of the 'older folk' would appear to believe every word of the tale he tells. His story is of Soulis learning the hard way that the community belief is true, and that contrary to Soulis's enlightened optimism, the devil is not 'mercifully restrained'. Folk superstition prevails, both in the clachan, and in Soulis's life, and for readers who simply want to enjoy a good ghost story. Stevenson, however, has produced something a little more complicated than that: ultimately, the credulous folk vision is kept at a distance by the tale's sense of writerly performance and Gothic improbability.

The strength of the tale, nevertheless, lies in its sheer vividness and its ability to entertain: it is one of the great Victorian ghost stories. And its success is clearly bound up with at least two features which are characteristic of Stevenson at his best: the tale is told through the consciousness and speech of a thoroughly characterized narrator, and its fictional substance is drawn from somewhere distinctly other than the everyday world of its contemporary readers.

TREASURE ISLAND (WRITTEN 1881)

Treasure Island provides an excellent illustration of how attitudes to Stevenson's essential genius have changed in recent decades. In an early important modern study of Stevenson's writing, David Daiches presented Stevenson as combining (in his personality as well as his writings) a 'boyish' (if brilliant) side and an 'adult' side, and suggested that his *oeuvre* can be understood as embodying a slow and scarcely completed journey of maturing from one to the other.

> So what we have already noted as an apparent conflict between a boyish and an adult strain in his character and writing is, in part at least, and from one point of view, the conflict between the romantic and the dramatic aspects of his art (to use Stevenson's terminology). There are, of course, other elements on both sides, but this is certainly one pair of different though not mutually exclusive factors in Stevenson's work. Stevenson was working towards a type of novel in which, while his sense of the picturesque could have full

scope, his sense of the genuinely dramatic could also operate. *The Master of Ballantrae* was an important step forward towards this ideal, but he made a bad mess of the latter part, where the novel slips completely out of the 'dramatic' category to bog down in a contrived romance which seems all the more artificial in the light of the dramatic kind of 'probability' established in the earlier part of the novel. In *Weir of Hermiston*, however, Stevenson's success is complete: the romantic elements in the novel add tremendously to the effectiveness of the essentially dramatic story without postulating a conflicting kind of probability. It was Stevenson's bad luck – and ours – that he should have perfected his art only at the moment of death.[11]

Thus the success of *Treasure Island*, which Daiches enthusiastically acknowledged, was seen, nevertheless, as a limited one: for true greatness it was necessary for Stevenson to move on from it. He and his writing had to grow up despite early brilliance and *Treasure Island*, it was implied, is to be both relished and not taken too seriously. Quite different is one of the most recent discussions of Stevenson, in Robert Crawford's *Scotland's Books*.[12] There, Stevenson's playfulness is seen and cherished as central to what makes him individual and important. We need not regret, it seems, that the author of *Treasure Island* was not George Eliot – let alone any of the tragic playwrights (Sophocles, Shakespeare) to whom Daiches referred. For Crawford, it is not simply that the thoroughly boyish fun of the pirate tale is to be celebrated on its own account. That playfulness of style and content becomes Stevenson's salvation.

> The pace and audience of *Treasure Island* demanded a curbing of Stevenson's 'fine writing', and in that curbing lay liberation. What is sometimes wrong with Stevenson's early work is that it strives too hard for a sophisticated 'Man of Letters' tone. His prose, like his best poetry, is often strongest when its language is both nuanced and most direct. That directness is linked to the author's deepest preoccupations, as in Stevenson's most famous poem, 'Requiem', which dates from early 1880:
>
> > *Home is the sailor, home from sea,*
> > *And the hunter home from the hill.*
>
> So it is with Stevenson's prose that around 1880–81 a shift takes place that rescues his writing from an excess of poise, and turns him towards purposeful play.[13]

Stevenson himself, in his own account of the writing of the book in his essay 'My First Book', makes much the same point about the liberation into directness which the book made possible – and necessary: 'It was to be a story for boys; no need of psychology or fine writing.'[14]

Hence the great paradox of *Treasure Island*: it is a 'boy's book' which grown-ups can, and do, read as seriously as they read literature written purely for themselves and their fellow adults. Stevenson himself provided a somewhat more complicated sketch of the writing, and nature, of *Treasure Island* in his earlier essay 'A Humble Remonstrance' where he insists (as he crosses friendly swords with Henry James) that grown-ups can enjoy such a book because they were once young. He believes that adults retain something of the imaginative freedoms of childhood. (Certainly, I find that I derive far more pleasure nowadays from re-reading *Treasure Island* than I can ever remember experiencing from it when I was first given a copy.)

Crawford's illuminating (if necessarily brief) account stresses how the book is deeply shaped by childhood imaginings and game-playing: '*Treasure Island* is a book not just to read but to play at. It is full of an energy that comes from play; from hide and seek, from boys' toys such as swords and boats, from fancy dress, from chases.'[15] With that point so well made, and with *Treasure Island*'s reputation as perhaps *the* archetypal children's classic, it is perhaps worth stressing here, rather, the adultness built into its imaginative qualities and its implications. If it evokes our recollections of our childhood imaginings, it strives to undercut and place them fairly exhaustively. The book takes the realm of boyhood's imaginative freedom as its starting-point, but instead of simply celebrating it *Treasure Island* equates that glorious boyish vision with an innocence which amounts to mere ignorance. The Jim Hawkins who arrives in Bristol and encounters a busy harbour for the first time embodies that vision:

> And I was going to sea myself; to sea in a schooner, with a piping boatswain, and pig-tailed singing seamen; to sea, bound for an unknown island, and to seek for buried treasures!
> While I was still in this delightful dream...[16]

The 'delightful dream' is no more than that and is inevitably interrupted – in this case by the slightly preposterous figure of Squire Trelawney 'all dressed out like a sea-officer' (*TI* 45). Trelawney is not only posturing and play-acting here, but embodying in himself the failure to fully grow up: he clearly shares Jim's excited boyish dreams, and as it turns out his innocence (in the form of complete guilelessness and an inability to foresee the dangers of an evil world focused by the prospect of treasure) is thoroughly dangerous. It has to be lost as soon as possible.

And that is what happens, to Trelawney, to Jim and to all the 'good' characters. Stevenson gets his characters to the island in record time, allotting the minimum of space to the voyage (which is the section of the tale in which the pirates are on their best behaviour, thus keeping intact Jim's boyish illusions) and making its one major episode, the adventure in the apple barrel, the revelation which shatters all those illusions. Nor is the island itself allowed even an initial glamour: its first brief description is muted and low-key. At their first anchorage, a place smelling of 'sodden leaves and rotting tree trunks' (*TI* 72), the doctor pronounces sourly, 'I don't know about treasure ... but I'll stake my wig there's fever here' (*TI* 73). Gazing at their goal, Silver attempts to stimulate a boyish response in Jim, not knowing that the boy now knows about his murderous perfidy: the pirate's bogus evocation of the island as a boy's playground is immediately undercut: '"Ah," says he, "this here is a sweet spot, this island – a sweet spot for a lad to get ashore on. You'll bathe, and you'll climb trees, and you'll hunt goats, you will; and you'll get aloft on them hills like a goat yourself. Why, it makes me young again".' (*TI* 67) The speaker's words are simultaneously negated by the very fact of the speaker himself, now known to be villainous: this is no boy's paradise and the first full description of the island scene, at the beginning of Chapter 13, culminates in Jim's instant revulsion: 'My heart sank, as the saying is, into my boots; and from that first look onward, I hated the very thought of Treasure Island.' (*TI* 71)

Jim's response is completely tied in with his physical perception of the place – he responds to the unexpectedly drab and weird appearance of the island with an equally unexpected and instant fixed loathing. In a way, the book is all about perception and Crawford is correct to see the fluctuating roles (and so, perceptions) of the reader – sometimes boyish, sometimes adult – as central to the book's nature. The characters' perceptions and judgements of one another, and the difficulty of arriving at true judgement, is an insistent motif. The excellent Captain Smollett is initially heartily disliked and despised by Trelawney and by Jim; Israel Hands is initially judged (ambiguously, it is true) to 'be trusted at a pinch with almost anything' (*TI* 57) by the cabin-boy who eventually has to shoot him in self-defence; the question of who in the crew is loyal to the squire's party and who is not is crucial both to the squire and his colleagues but also to the pirates. Above all, of course, there is the issue of Long John Silver, for long seen as the most trustworthy of the crew (till Jim's apple-barrel revelation) and the usual focus for discussions of Stevenson's treatment (at least so far as this novel is concerned) of his recurring theme of doubleness. Here, the two-sidedness of Silver is purely part and parcel of his dangerous villainy – he has an almost preternatural ability to deceive. His ability to make himself endearing does not mean that he is, in fact, an endearing character, despite Stevenson's somewhat tight-lipped acknowledgement in 'My First Book' that 'to this day [I] rather admire that smooth and formidable adventurer'[17]; rather, it indicates that he is kin to the Father of Lies and, more immediately, to that later embodiment of the Stevensonian devil, James Durie.

The principal doubleness of the book lies elsewhere, in its fluctuations between boyishness and adult maturity – both as regards its own nature, as already mentioned, and as regards the implied reader. This is a matter to which writers on Stevenson still regularly return. Alan Riach, for example, meditates on the mystery of its success in satisfying male readers of all ages.[18] Biographers of Stevenson, and commentators on the book, regularly point out the importance of the circumstances of its creation, with Stevenson spinning his yarn to entertain ((primarily) both a young lad, Lloyd Osbourne, and an elderly gentleman, his own father. The present-day reader needs to bring both modes of perception to the book and it may be that a child's sensibility alone cannot properly respond to the work – though it would seem perverse to decide that this is essentially a book for adults only! Oliver S. Buckton has developed the implications of the novel's origins, particularly with regard to the crucial emergence of the famous map which played such an important part in helping entertain the family during the holiday downpours at Braemar: the tale, he argues, entertained thereafter not only Lloyd Osbourne and Thomas Stevenson but a whole new readership of adult males who have found pleasure in reverting to the condition of boyhood in their imaginations.[19] Indeed, (argues Buckton), Stevenson's fashioning of this particular readership had wide implications for the emerging concept of empire and imperial service, as a realm of specifically masculine adventure and idealism.

Be that as it may, it does not require our knowledge of Stevenson's complex relationship with his own father to see that the heart of the book lies in the relationship of Jim Hawkins and Long John Silver: boyhood and adulthood together form the essential framework for the tale. One can summarize by saying that *Treasure Island* is the story of a boy's encounter with the danger, the evil and the sheer complexity of the adult world, a world to some extent distilled in the person of Silver. Jim is essentially, as we meet him, without his own father from the start, though the parent's actual death takes place off-stage in Chapter 3 amid all the growing excitement of the pirates closing in on Billy Bones. A hint of fatherhood, *vis-à-vis* Jim, lingers around Bones himself despite (or indeed, perhaps, because of) his domineering ways; certainly, Jim's spontaneous response to his death matches that of a son for a father, as Jim is at least half aware: 'It is a curious thing to understand, for I had certainly never liked the man, though of late I had begun to pity him, but as soon as I saw that he was dead, I burst into a flood of tears. It was the second death I had known, and the sorrow of the first was still fresh in my heart.' (*TI* 24) One has to take Jim's sorrow for his real father's death a little for granted as it is not dwelt upon – not that the growing piratical threat seems to give him much opportunity for quiet mourning. Instead, his father's death is merely one of the sudden flurry of events which propel him into new realms of experience. It is one example of how Stevenson pared down the potential complexities of his characters and their situations (as he describes in 'A Humble Remonstrance') that the recently bereaved Jim is allowed (by the author and by us) to leap into the excitement of the treasure quest untrammelled by emotional disturbance.

To focus on the duality of Jim and Silver risks making the novel sound as if it is an exploration of Innocence and Experience. Not that Jim makes any elaborate, sustained transition from one to the other in the course of the story, nor do we have a particularly powerful sense of the older Jim, narrating the tale, as vastly more experienced in life than his younger adventurous self. Jim's attitudes and insights, after the episode of the apple barrel at least, are broadly fixed and to be relied upon, so that it is not the tale of a boy's growing up: as we have seen, he is instinctively horrified by the island as soon as he sees it properly and his time there, from the start, is spent (merely) surviving and counter-plotting against the known danger of Silver and his men. He does not mature on the island; rather, he survives and contributes signally to the triumph of good over evil. Indeed, it is his apparently immature, boyish behaviour which paradoxically proves decisive. Twice he gives in to the thoughtless impulse of a young scallywag and slips away on his own, from the ship when the pirate crew is first allowed on shore and from the stockade after the pirate attack. This latter escapade is thoroughly reprehensible, as the adult Jim (narrating the novel) admits: 'But I was only a boy, and I had made my mind up.' (*TI* 117) Jim makes no visible progress towards a mature (and so, presumably, conventionally effective) way of responding to life's serious challenges: rather, it is his boyish thoughtlessness which contributes, in a major way, to the happy outcome. There is clear justification, therefore, for reading the novel as a boy's daydream – as a fantasy in which it is one's very youthful impulsiveness and irresponsibility which brings about triumph. Indeed, not only does Jim blurt out his successes in defiance of the pirates who have captured him ('The laugh's on my side; I've had the top of this business from the first' etc (*TI* 148)) but the doctor, too, contemplates the strangely decisive role that Jim's youthfully irresponsible behaviour has played: 'There is a kind of fate in this...Every step, it's you that saves our lives.' (*TI* 161) Jim's last comment on himself appears, at first glance, to represent a more mature outlook ('The bar silver and the arms still lie, for all that I know, where Flint buried them; and certainly they shall lie there for me. Oxen and wain-ropes would not bring me back again to that accursed island' (*TI* 183)), but even this can be interpreted as reflecting the attitude of a pre-adult with a set of values which has no place for the pure acquisitiveness which has motivated nearly all the adult characters in the book.

Jim's boyishness, therefore, is an embodiment of righteous innocence. Consequently, it becomes all the more piquant that the action climaxes in pairing him, in a struggle of mutual survival, with his diametrical opposite, Silver. If, as readers, we end sharing something of Stevenson's soft spot for Silver, it is partly because he has been aligned, at the phase of maximum danger for Jim, with the young hero, confronting the same threats and contributing to his eventual escape. If Jim embodies the daydream of innocent and righteous youth granted a near-magical power in countering, surviving, and overcoming evil (his distant literary kin surely include Frodo Baggins and Harry Potter), Silver is simply the opposite: 'experienced' in life to the extent of murder – thus knowing all that fallen humanity might know and being all that fallen humanity (Cain-like) might be. That he is not simply rejected by us as a villain is due to the fact that his total knowledge of human experience is inextricably entwined with a seemingly boundless courage, resourcefulness, and ability to make himself seem whatever he wants. Consequently, his zest for life itself seems unbounded, and in his masterly duplicity he also fascinates. That the key to Silver is 'experience' (the total knowledge of human life in all its aspects) is further suggested by that iconic appendage which, with his single leg, makes him so visible to us and thus so powerfully present in our imaginations – his parrot.

> 'Now, that bird,' he would say, 'is, may be, two hundred years old, Hawkins – they lives for ever mostly; and if anybody's seen more wickedness, it must be the devil himself. She's sailed with England, the great Cap'n England, the pirate. She's been at Madagascar, and at Malabar, and Surinam, and Providence, and Portobello. She was at the fishing up of the wrecked plate ships. It's there she learned "Pieces of eight," and little wonder; three hundred and fifty thousand of 'em, Hawkins! She was at the boarding of the Viceroy of the Indies out of Goa, she was; and to look at her you would think she was a babby.' (*TI* 58)

And this feathered experience is combined (duality again) with a complete innocence, the parrot 'swearing blue fire, and none the wiser' (*TI* 58). Does some of that paradoxical combination rub off on to Silver, or at least on to our response to him? Certainly, the parrot distils much that is both entertaining and terrible in the piratical world into which Jim has been plunged, just as its cry of 'Pieces of eight!' combines both the magical allure and the terrifying greed of the pirate quest. If Jim has learned anything about life as a result of his island adventure, it appears to be summed up, somewhat gnomically, in the famous cry of the parrot which constitutes the book's last word.

The mystery of Stevenson's book is finally embodied in Silver, so utterly charming and appealing to Jim (and us) while Jim's vision is untainted by a sense of evil and danger, so murderously ruthless in the context of Jim's knowledge of the reality of the pirates. In a way, his very presence in the book makes it a book for adults: no purely child's book could contain his capacity for viciousness. He is a type of character Stevenson uses elsewhere, in works which are more clearly aimed at grown-ups: he is followed in duplicity and ruthlessness by the Master of Ballantrae, for example, and for each fascinating villain Stevenson devises a narrative climax involving a display of wits and courage as he strives to stay alive surrounded by threatening desperadoes. In a way, the ambiguous response we have to characters of this type is possible only in adventure romances of the kind which Stevenson is writing in these books, for in them physical courage, audacity, and steely nerves become attributes to be highly prized and their possessors seem inevitably heroic.

The continued readability and fascination of *Treasure Island*, then, seems bound up with its refusal to be pinned down while offering, on the surface, a reading-experience of attractive clarity, directness, and freshness. Stevenson's abandonment of 'fine writing' releases the book's unobtrusive vividness which, in itself, contributes so much. Its writing is marked by an apparently simple fusing of words and imagined reality. It has a narrative clarity and simplicity which is not confined merely to the speedy flow of the story (important as that is) but is also felt in Stevenson's physical descriptions and, perhaps most crucially of all, in the vividness of unfolding situations: see, for example, his account of the detailed movements of the drifting *Hispaniola* when Jim sneaks aboard from the coracle in the final paragraphs of Chapter 24 and the first few of Chapter 25. At such moments, the success of the intense simplicity of *Treasure Island* is clear – a simplicity which might appear to be a mere concession to youthful readers but which is also part of its appeal to adults.

Stevenson has created a novel for children which, if anything, is even more a novel for adults. It works by undermining and denying a vision of childish adventure which, at first glance (and in its reputation), it seems to embody with complete success and conviction. Pirates and treasure-hunting, and everything implied by the island-world itself, are to be mistrusted and shunned, although their necessity as part of our maturing imaginations is acknowledged by the very existence of the book. Jim Hawkins is the triumphantly innocent hero of boyhood games and of other writers' less subtle boyish literature, but he is also the embodiment of the mature realization that the world contains no dangers from which we are miraculously secure. Jim is both innocent and the loser of innocence, even as his island adventures proceed. A similar ambiguity extends both to Silver (attractive as boyhood's exotic conception of piracy, but repellent as its murderous reality) and also to the reader, asked to be now a child, and now a grown-up. The novel's settings, too, have something of the same duality. Not only is the island a boy's adventure playground as well as a dank, depressing domain of wholly unattractive villainy but even its opposite, the domestic world of the West Country inn, represents both the un-exotic ordinariness of 'home' and (for readers of both Stevenson's century and our own) an exotic 'literary' environment from which romantic adventure can easily flower. In this book, the most diverse opposites fuse and co-exist: Silver's parrot, utterly innocent in its foul-mouthed experience of the world, is its perfect symbol.

The novel seems such an excellent example of Stevenson's graceful genius as a writer that it seems ironic that soon after his death there was some controversy as to whether he had been influenced by an earlier (now forgotten) sea-going novel. Glenda Norquay reminds us of how sensitive Stevenson's friends were to the suggestion that *Treasure Island* might have been anything other than the product of spontaneous artistic inspiration.[20] The issue had nothing to do with plagiarism, and everything to do with opposing concepts of the writing process: in our present-day terminology, was *Treasure Island* to be seen as a literary fiction emerging from mysterious creative energy, or merely as a popular fiction consciously written to a formula – the writer as a genius or a workman? (We surely need not assume that the two are incompatible, of course: the friends were undoubtedly right in feeling that there is a generous touch of genius about the novel, but Stevenson himself would have been perfectly conscious of his predecessors in writing sea-going adventures for children, predecessors such as R. M. Ballantyne, Captain Marryat, Captain Mayne Reid, and Daniel Defoe himself.) Other critics have also helped locate this seemingly ever-present work in its historical setting. Julia Reid, for example, sees it not only as an example of romance writing, but also as an expression of doubt about the implications of romance itself, thanks to the associations which had developed between tales of sea-adventures and the need to bolster the national self-image at a time of decreasing British self-confidence and security.[21] Jim's doubts about the island, and about treasure-hunting, might be reflecting doubts about imperialism itself and the heroic manliness which it required. Joseph Bristow is equally conscious of the underlying imperialism in the classic nine-teenth-century island-adventure stories, though he is also concerned with *Treasure Island* and its place in one of the literary controversies of its day: can fiction be a domain for men as well as for the women who seemed to be forming the great bulk of the late Victorian reading public? And Bristow falls in with most present-day discussions of the place of *Treasure Island* in its time by finally focusing on the issue of romance versus realism as modes of fiction.[22] It can seem paradoxical that this apparently most headlong tale of adventure for boyish readers should so consistently raise matters of literary theory, but perhaps all one need respond is 'Well, Stevenson and Henry James started it!'.

'THE TREASURE OF FRANCHARD' (WRITTEN 1882)

In outline, the story of 'The Treasure of Franchard' might seem unpromising, an attempt at whimsical comedy, with its slight, improbable narrative and its happy-ever-after ending. Desprez, a French provincial doctor, and his wife Anastasie adopt (though in no formal way) an abandoned nine-year-old waif,

Jean-Marie; the discovery of a treasure-hoard offers them a momentary glimpse of escape from the provinces but the boy, fearful of the destructive effect of Parisian sophistication on their essentially contented lives, hides the booty. After this calamity, yet more: almost simultaneously, their ancient house collapses in a gale and the doctor's foolish investments evaporate. Will Jean-Marie, his comfortable billet thus wrecked, reveal his true colours and abandon them? For a moment it seems that he has – until he returns with the loot he had previously stashed away. Relief, joy, and contentment all round.

In fact, this is one of Stevenson's short-story successes, a genuinely entertaining and individual piece which manages to draw on some of its author's important strengths. Its slightness encourages modern critics to largely ignore it, but it forms an important and effective part of *The Merry Men and Other Tales* which Stevenson eventually published in 1887. This collection contains material first published in periodicals between 1878 and 1885 – 'The Treasure of Franchard' had appeared in *Longman's Magazine* in 1883, having been turned down by the *Cornhill* as 'unfit for a family magazine'. This judgement seems bizarre, at first sight, but it gives a distant clue to at least part of what is distinctive and successful about the story. Whimsically unlikely and comic as the tale may be, it reflects, in its mannered way, Stevenson's realistic sense of human and cultural realities: he knows (and loves) the kind of people he is writing about, and he is taking an un-idealized but warmly tolerant view of their failings. This includes an awareness of their sexuality and allows him to make comic capital out of a married woman's night-attire modesty during the hair's-breadth escape from the collapsing building. Not that Stevenson offers anything remotely salacious (at least by our standards), but he is writing with a confident freedom which arises, finally, from his complete success here in fusing style, matter, and view of life. There is a unity of conception and effect which is typical of Stevenson at his best and which helps highlight those other occasions when, frankly, it fails to come off.

As so often in Stevenson, the success is bound up with the quality and nature of the writing itself. There are two dimensions of the story's prose to consider, namely the narration and also the high-flown speech which is central to the characterization of Dr Desprez. The opening words demonstrate the confident vigour with which the narrator unfolds the tale:

> They had sent for the doctor from Bourron before six. About eight some villagers came round for the performance, and were told how matters stood. It seemed a liberty for a mountebank to fall ill like real people, and they made off again in dudgeon. By ten Madame Tentaillon was gravely alarmed, and had sent down the street for Doctor Desprez. (VII, TF 191)

The promise, here, of speed and clarity in the telling, combined with a dry irony ('It seemed a liberty for a mountebank to fall ill like real people') is fulfilled by the rest of the tale, and proves ideal for a story of well-observed humble provincial life (French, admittedly) built around a series of somewhat improbable occurrences. It is one of Stevenson's evocations of life in the vicinity of Fontainebleau, where he had found liberation (and Fanny) several years earlier. The simple ordinariness of life in such an environment, so relaxed in contrast to the tensions of Stevenson's life in the bosom of the family in Edinburgh, is in a sense what the story is about; this is the quality which claims and encloses the central characters and which the wise little boy, almost a holy fool, prizes so consciously and so decisively. What the irony evokes is Stevenson's role as external observer (in real life as well as in his writing) and also his amusement at the self-deception of, above all, Desprez himself. The irony also expresses the down-to-earth common sense which is the human value espoused by the story. Common sense is a quality which Doctor Desprez, the central character, manages (in his Stevensonian duality) both to embody and to lack. Vocally, the doctor is an endearing humbug, loud in his philosophical proclamations of the health-filled virtues of the local way of life but secretly eager, as events reveal, to abandon healthy rural simplicity for the expensive delights of the world's most fashionable city. His characteristically flamboyant language embodies his pretensions but also makes him endearing ('that gentleman never wearied of the sound of his own voice, which was, to say the truth, agreeable enough to hear' (TF 213)), as when he explains the legend that there is treasure secreted in the tract of country where he and Jean-Marie are heading (to collect plants) and as he contemplates the fact that it has never yet been found:

> 'You have no imagination,' cried the Doctor. 'Picture to yourself the scene. Dwell on the idea – a great treasure lying in the earth for centuries: the material for a giddy, copious, opulent existence not employed; dresses and exquisite pictures unseen; the swiftest galloping horses not stirring a hoof, arrested by a spell; women with the beautiful faculty of smiles, not smiling; cards, dice, opera singers, orchestras, castles, beautiful parks and gardens, big ships with a tower of sailcloth, all lying unborn in a coffin – and the stupid trees growing overhead in the sunlight, year after year. The thought drives one frantic.' (TF 224–5)

The treasure is found, miraculously, and then lost as swiftly, an episode which demonstrates Desprez's silliness and wisdom in equal measure, for he cannot see the obvious truth staring him in the face – Jean-Marie has taken it. Yet within this foolish blindness there is wisdom: he is correct to believe the boy incapable of theft. The treasure has been removed through the best, not the worst, of intentions and the 'theft' proves to be the saving of the family in the end.

The potential for sentimentality here is high, and not all readers may feel it has been avoided. The 'message' of contentment with a humble lot, with the provincialism of commonplace things, and with everyday love and family life, could have been merely trite. That it is not is due to the very lack of pretension in the conception and method of the story: in this it contrasts with another of the tales in the collection, 'Will o' the Mill'. One's doubts about how to read that story are not repeated in the case of 'The Treasure of Franchard'. Its message of contentment with the simple basics of life may feel somewhat at odds with our knowledge of Stevenson's own eagerness to experience what the world has to offer, and his willingness to travel to the ends of the earth. Yet the conventional little world of the doctor and his wife is clearly the right one for them and, in any case, Desprez has made at least one bold spring into the unknown by suddenly adopting Jean-Marie in the first place, an impulse derived from the everyday good-heartedness and generosity which convincingly underlies all his flim-flam. His rootedness is convincing, where Will's seems merely puzzling, perverse, and disquieting.

One suspects, too, that in one of its aspects 'The Treasure of Franchard' is an amused portrait of Stevenson's own marriage. Desprez may not travel like the Stevensons, but his endlessly creative verbalism makes him a kind of artist and his efforts are certainly entertaining, despite their pointlessness. Anastasie, in contrast, is a fount of good sense although she is also a legitimate object of amusement in her wifely decorousness. Contented matrimony here finds convincing expression, not least in the frequent hint that sexuality is a pleasure, a comfort, and a central part of their life together, even though their marital badinage is sometimes coloured by the hinted possibility that Desprez might choose to be unfaithful. Perhaps this was the feature which caused the problem for the *Cornhill*. Or perhaps it was the image of the family stranded in their night-attire. Or perhaps the particular difficulty was the loss of the doctor's trousers in the collapse of the house. Their eventual re-discovery, ruined, gives rise to a lament of Pythonesque comedy: 'The Doctor ruefully took it in his hands. "They have been!" he said. "Their tense is past. Excellent pantaloons, you are no more!" ' (TF 256) 'The Treasure of Franchard' may not be serious in its manner, yet it does carry a theme which recurs, unobtrusively, in much of Stevenson's writing, namely the choice between its two alternative lifestyles. Desprez, perennially glorying in the simplicity of his provincial domesticity but momentarily revealed as longing, with at least part of his being, for the bright lights of Paris, projects the theme with a simple clarity. But much of Stevenson's work, from *New Arabian Nights* to *Weir of Hermiston*, sets these two domains in opposition. In one direction, we can see this as related to the perennial dualism of realism and romance which is the condition of his fiction; in another direction, we can associate it with the real life-style choice that he made. The South Sea retreat and the establishment of a family home at Vailima came about primarily for reasons of health, but also enabled Stevenson to combine domesticity with the romance of the distant and the exotic. So, in his stories, the life of quiet retirement, whether it be that of Florizel in his tobacco shop, or Desborough and Clara (in *The Dynamiter*), or Dick Shelton and his Joan, or Otto and Seraphina, or indeed of Henry Durie at Ballantrae, is frequently to be found within the larger context of their romance tales. And so it is with

Desprez's Gretz: Stevenson cannot avoid making French provincial life, apparently a world of bohemian hedonism with its delicious food and wine, appear to English-speaking readers to be as desirable and escapist an alternative to their mundane and responsible existences as might be conjured up.

PRINCE OTTO: A ROMANCE (WRITTEN 1883)

Prince Otto has always troubled readers: contemporary reviewers disliked it or were disappointed in it and it had little of the immediate success of *Treasure Island*; critics today dismiss it and it is now largely ignored. Yet all who encounter it agree that no one but Stevenson could have written it, and for Stevenson himself it represented an especial effort. That effort was not simply a matter of repeated drafting and re-drafting but was also an attempt at achieving what he himself could regard as an artistic success embodying his by now well-worked-out ideas of literary excellence. At first, he was inclined to blame the public, and various reviewers, for not appreciating the pearl he was casting before them, though as time went by he acknowledged that the book itself was at fault. 'Otto was my hardest effort, for I wished to do something very swell, which did not quite come off,' he wrote to George Iles on 29 October 1887 (Mehew 349).

Set in a tiny central European Ruritanian kingdom in a somewhat indeterminate period of history, it puzzles the reader in various ways. What is it about? What are we to make of its central characters, the good-hearted but ineffectual and irresponsible Otto above all? What sort of novel is it, with its strong overtones of light romantic comedy curiously matched with an attempt to handle weightier matters of politics and sexuality? In his essay of the following year, 'A Humble Remonstrance', Stevenson would insist that it was the task of the artist to create works in which all elements contributed to an overall design or goal:

> From all its chapters, from all its pages, from all its sentences, the well-written novel echoes and re-echoes its one creative and controlling thought; to this must every incident and character contribute; the style must have been pitched in unison with this; and

37

if there is anywhere a word that looks another way, the book would be stronger, clearer, and (I had almost said) fuller without it.[23]

His comments about *Prince Otto*, in his letter to Gosse of 2 January 1886, breathe the same air of aesthetic idealism as he contemplates the lukewarm reception which had rewarded his efforts: 'You aim high, and you take longer over your work; and it will not be so successful as if you had aimed low and rushed it.' (Mehew 299) But few readers, one suspects, can have been confident in discerning *Prince Otto*'s 'one creative and controlling thought'; once later and more coherent works had emerged from his pen, one wonders how many readers have really tried.

It has to be admitted that Stevenson always seems to know where he wants the narrative to go, and this despite his usual habit of working scene by scene, episode by episode. Even his later and greater novels consist essentially of a series of vividly realized moments, and retain their kinship with his short stories and with *New Arabian Nights*. In *Prince Otto*, most chapters bring a fresh focus, a fresh setting, a different combination of characters, yet Stevenson makes his story unfold confidently; the problem does not lie there. Mainly, it lies in Otto himself and in the question of why Stevenson is interested in him. Equally, despite the book's clear awareness of serious adult concerns, Stevenson elected to write of his Ruritanian world in a style which deliberately embraces the artificial (as he wrote to Henley in early May 1883, 'the unreality [of an Arabian Night] is there and the classic pomp' while the characters 'all talk like books – none of your colloquial wash' (Mehew 223)). The result is an instability which few find satisfying. Commentators with a marked biographical interest in Stevenson see the book as particularly revealing ('in one form or another, the three greatest influences in his life – Bob, Fanny and his father – all make an appearance'); others simply see in it Stevenson's misconceived first attempt at a novel for adults.[24]

Yet however painfully laborious it may have been to write, Stevenson did not appear to feel that it was his conception which was at fault, and there is indeed a harmony between the effete, ineffective but essentially noble Otto and the story-book world of his tiny kingdom of Grünewald. The clue is perhaps in the name: the world of this book is that of the greenwood – in the double sense that it offers itself as a fictional world which eschews everyday realism, and also in that the tale contrasts the worlds of court and greenwood in a way which may well be a deliberate echo of *As You Like It*, a particular favourite of Stevenson's. 'In early adulthood he conceived a love for *As You Like It* which never died.'[25] The novel opens and closes in the forest, where Otto is first seen taking advantage of a hunt to ride in total freedom till nightfall, characteristically turning his back on his responsibilities: the governing of the principality has devolved upon the ambitious and capable minister, Gondremark, and upon Seraphina, Otto's young wife. She is rumoured (mistakenly) to be Gondremark's mistress. The tale, as it develops, focuses upon the relationship between the irresponsible (and sexually unimpressive) husband and the immature but confident and capable wife who has directed her energies into ruling the kingdom. Firm rule is necessary, because republican revolution threatens to break out. The crudely effective and Machiavellian Gondremark, at Seraphina's right-hand, aims to take advantage of this instability by attacking a neighbouring state and uniting Grünewald under his own leadership. (Bismarck certainly lurks in the background here.) The crisis comes when Gondremark's real mistress, Countess von Rosen, gives Seraphina some insight into Otto's true worth and also into the extent to which he still loves his wife. At the same time, Gondremark's duplicity is laid before her and in the ensuing impassioned argument with the scheming minister, Seraphina stabs him (she thinks, fatally) thereby precipitating the long-threatened revolution. Fleeing through the forest, Seraphina makes her way to the castle from whence the imprisoned Otto has just been released and, freed at last from the cares and responsibilities of state, the pair re-start their marriage locked in a teasingly ambiguous embrace, lying alone together on 'a lawn among the forest, very green and innocent, and solemnly surrounded by trees' (IV, *PO* 298). Hymen reigns – unlike the now dispossessed, but happier, Otto and Seraphina. It is all very far from island treasure, flights in the heather, or murderous, brotherly *alter egos*.

Just as *As You Like It* explores real human relationships and desires refined and made apparently chaste in the green world of Arden, so Grünewald enables Stevenson to portray his characters as sexual beings with a greater measure of openness than ever before or, with very few exceptions, than he would ever approach again. Although by modern standards still heavily veiled, *Prince Otto* is notable for the directness with which it contemplates the possibility that its heroine has been physically unfaithful to her husband, and with which it explores an unhappy marriage in partially sexual terms. Stevenson's consciousness of writing of sex with a measure of intoxicating freedom is particularly clearly conveyed in his description of von Rosen, in that same letter to Henley, as 'a jolly, elderly – how shall I say? – fuckstress' (Mehew 223), and the swift strokes with which he sketches the relaxed licentiousness of the Gondremark/von Rosen relationship, however tame by the standards of other ages, are noteworthy in the context of Stevenson's writing.

Arresting also is the novel's political dimension. That said, it is possible to over-dignify the political world of *Prince Otto*, which scarcely attains even the immediacy of the whimsical treatment of Fenianism in *The Dynamiter* of the following year. True, republicanism is given its voice in Otto's encounter with the family of Killian Gottesheim in Chapter 2, and its authoritarian opposite is explored in his discussion with Roederer in Chapter 4, but neither exchange is sufficiently weighty to elevate the book's political strand to seriousness. Rather, Stevenson's treatment of the politics of Grünewald is a matter of personalities and plot externals. It is as if he were taking his cue from Shakespeare once more, from the English history plays and *Measure for Measure*. Otto's kinship, also, with the indecisive and ineffectual Hamlet of Romantic tradition is regularly commented upon. In addition, the opening of *Prince Otto* confirms one's suspicions, aroused by the choice of 'Florizel' for the name of the prince of *New Arabian Nights*, that *The Winter's Tale* forms part of the imaginative background to Stevenson's early writings: 'Several intermarriages had, in the course of centuries, united the crowned families of Grünewald and Maritime Bohemia; and the last Prince of Grünewald... drew his descent through Perdita, the only daughter of King Florizel the First of Bohemia.' (IV, *PO* 98)

The political strand of the novel is not, it would seem, of interest to Stevenson in itself. Rather, it embodies one pole of the more personal issue which was of far greater moment to him as a writer, namely the conflict between effective involvement in the practical affairs of the world (such as building lighthouses) and apparently selfish, idle, and unimportant dilettantism (inventing stories?). Here, surely, is at least part of what the novel is really about. While almost all the other characters condemn Otto's irresponsibility to a greater or lesser extent, the most weighty criticism is put into the words of an English traveller, Sir John Crabtree, whose stinging account of the court of Grünewald forms a complete early chapter. In part, the book's progress is from the harshness of Sir John's summary of the public's perception of the royal pair (voiced with the confident forth-rightness of Victorian England – Otto is 'a young man of imperfect education, questionable valour, and no scintilla of capacity' while Seraphina is 'sick with vanity, superficially clever, and fundamentally a fool... Hoyden playing Cleopatra' (*PO* 149, 150)) to his eventual personal sympathy with, and liking for them. In the end, the health of the nation is apparently of less consequence than the health of the personal life, and if the young couple's rule is botched we are asked to rejoice that their marriage is patched. Eventually, Otto and Seraphina each discover who they are in themselves, and what is valuable in the other. The court world, corrupt and corrupting in the manner of fairy-tales and of Shakespearean romance, has concealed what is best and most true in them. Their reconciliation demands honesty from them both, an honesty which emerges as a moral responsibility which substitutes for their moral failures as rulers.

In an unfamiliar guise, a Stevensonian motif emerges here. Where in later and more famous works doubleness is promi-nent, here it is more transparently treated – in part because it takes that most familiar of narrative forms, the emerging love of a man and a woman. Yet Otto and Seraphina must take their place with later pairings: Alan and David, the Duries, Jekyll and Hyde. In each case, opposites are thirled together, either to clash irreconcilably or to work their way to mutual understanding, respect, and harmony. The Romantic 'fall into division' always produces conflict, tension, and sometimes total disaster, but it also produces the stuff of stories: conflict, tension, and total disaster or eventual harmony are what we want a storyteller to offer us.

Perhaps the problem with *Prince Otto* is that Stevenson is too much the storyteller, and that his belief that novels are rightly and essentially distanced from 'life' is too overwhelming. It is as if the opinions of 'A Humble Remonstrance' were being carried too far, and their one-sidedness inadvertently and prematurely demonstrated: 'The novel, which is a work of art, exists, not by its resemblances to life, which are forced and material, as a shoe must still consist of leather, but by its immeasurable difference from life, which is designed and significant, and is both the method and the meaning of the work.'[26] *Prince Otto* looks as if it has been concocted not from a sense of life, but from a sense of literature. As already indicated, Shakespeare seems everywhere in it, but so does the fairy-tale or folk-tale (with several chapter-titles underlining the fairy-tale quality – 'In Which the Prince Plays Haroun-Al-Raschid'; 'Princess Cinderella'; 'Babes in the Wood'). His favourite Dumas lurks also. And the literary artifice eventually explodes in the final 'Bibliographical Postscript To Complete the Story'(*PO* 301–3), where Stevenson returns to the mode of the opening: 'Perdita, the only daughter of King Florizel of Bohemia', with his elaborate spoof references to 'historical' works on Grünewald ('the memoirs of Herr Greisengesang (7 Bände: Leipzig)', 'the vigorous and bracing pages of Sir John (2 vols.: London: Longman, Hurst, Rees, Orme and Brown)') and to several other transparently jokey publications. In this novel, literary artifice is imposed upon reality rather than emerging from it. We may choose to regret that Stevenson, on this occasion, preferred to make his characters talk like books: a thorough scrubbing in 'your colloquial wash' might have spared us much stilted dialogue. Yet Stevenson was such a chameleon in devising styles to suit the variety of his tales that it is not to be wondered at that a flawed conception is expressed, for once, in flawed language.

THE BLACK ARROW (WRITTEN 1883)

The Black Arrow was written rapidly, to be serialized in *Young Folks* just as *Treasure Island* had been (under the title *The Sea Cook*). It is startling to realize that of the two novels, it was *The Black Arrow* which had by far the greater appeal to the young folks buying the periodical, for its circulation shot up in a way it had never done in response to Stevenson's pirates. Nowadays, *The Black Arrow* is generally regarded as one of Stevenson's also-ran publications. Some modern biographers fail to discuss it at any length while more extended accounts stress its flaws, only occasionally allowing it counterbalancing virtues. Stevenson himself was famously dismissive, in letters to Henley (late May 1883) and Colvin (early November 1883): 'a whole tale of tushery. And every tusher tushes me so free, that may I be tushed if the whole thing is worth a tush. "The Black Arrow: A Tale of Tunstall Forest" is his name: tush! a poor thing!' (Mehew 225n.) Yet he did not disown it entirely. It is a tale of the Wars of the Roses and he welcomed, in a telling phrase, the opportunity to bring Richard Crookback (the future Richard III) into his fiction: 'I am pleased you like Crookback; he is a fellow whose hellish energy has always fixed my attention.' And he hinted at the possibility of returning to the novel's basic idea at a later date: 'Some day, I will re-tickle the Sable Missile, and shoot it, *moyennant finances*, once more into the air; I can lighten it of much, and devote some more attention to Dick o' Gloucester. It's great sport to write tushery.' (Mehew 238) 'Tushery', Stevenson's coinage, refers to the pseudo-archaic language he adopts for his dialogue in this novel and the author's cheerful disdain for it is likely to be matched by the modern reader's sad amusement:

> 'Why, now, what aileth thee?' said Dick. 'Me-thinks I help you very patently. But my heart is sorry for so spiritless a fellow! And see ye here, John Matcham – sith John Matcham is your name – I, Richard Shelton, tide what betideth, come what may, will see you safe in Holywood. The saints so do to me again if I default you. Come, pick me up a good heart, Sir White-face. The way betters here; spur me the horse.' (VIII, *BA* 35–6)

Stevenson is particularly reliant upon the so-called ethic dative ('Where goeth me this track?') in his attempts to create an impression of fifteenth-century speech, but whereas in real life this construction was used only occasionally to suggest a relaxed intimacy between speakers, Stevenson makes it a defining and dominant feature of his characters' linguistic world. The falsity of Stevenson's 'tushery' is, one suspects, one of the principal reasons why modern critics regard the novel as weak. (Modern critics – though perhaps not modern readers: *The Black Arrow*

43

still appears in a healthy and diverse number of modern editions. It is possible, though, that this is due primarily to the opportunity to entice readers by combining Stevenson's name with striking cover-art.) Certainly the often hilarious dialogue is one of the ways in which (to our eyes) *The Black Arrow* suffers so much in contrast to *Treasure Island*. One of the most striking aspects of that earlier achievement was Stevenson's dialogue, especially in the creation of Long John Silver. Stagey as it may be, Silver's speech reads as if it had been really heard by Stevenson, whereas speech in *The Black Arrow* carries no overtones other than those of the library. That it is clearly the product of much linguistic effort and exploration by Stevenson only heightens our sense of its artifice. Inadvertently, it underlines how important it was to Stevenson, and to his chances of artistic success, that he found for each novel an appropriate dialogue style, for it is one of his most interesting characteristics that dialogue contributes to each work more than its normal proportion of weight to the final artistic impact. Here, unfortunately, 'fine writing' metamorphoses into an even more elaborately artificial 'historical' mode. Obviously, Stevenson's principal precursor and model was the Scott of *Ivanhoe*, a novel which has to negotiate a similar uneasy compromise between the appearance of medieval English and the accessibility of nineteenth-century conversation. Like Stevenson, Scott sprinkles his dialogue with putative medieval references, attempting to conjure a world-awareness pre-dating the present by many centuries. Yet Scott's fustian style seems less obtrusive than Stevenson's, for he was simply less of a stylist than the later writer. Stevenson's very strengths work against him here: when such a vigorous stylist miscalculates, the result has a luridness which the linguistically paler writer avoids, and the perverse zest with which he concocts the dialogue ('it's great sport to write tushery') makes him all the more committed to a misconceived goal.

The vigour with which Stevenson writes his supposedly 'historical' dialogue is matched by the various indications that fidelity to the period, as he conceived it, was important to him and something he wished, gently, to parade. This desire is visible, for example, in his insistence on calling the projectile fired from a crossbow a 'quarrel', rather than a 'bolt': both terms are correct and 'quarrel' was still a known usage in Victorian English, yet 'bolt' now seems the obvious word. An online search suggests that Scott, in *Ivanhoe*, always used 'bolt', never 'quarrel'. And perhaps we should not find it surprising that Stevenson's 'fidelity to the period' results in the staginess which pervades the novel, for he is writing during a period in which theatre productions of historical drama – in particular, Shakespeare's – were characterized by attempts at a historical realism resulting in stage pictures of elaborate detail. Stevenson was drawn, for many a year, to the theatre, trying continually to write a successful play, usually in collaboration with either Henley or with Lloyd Osbourne, and had contacts with both Henry Irving and Beerbohm Tree, the dominant forces in the English theatre of the time and both greatly wedded to the ideal of historical accuracy. It seems safe to assume that Stevenson's concept of historicity in literature was at least partly influenced by their stagings.

The language of *The Black Arrow* is only the most obvious of its weaknesses – perhaps one which bothers us more than it did the book's first readers. Other problems relate to the structure and to the conduct of the narrative. Stevenson pays the price for the haste (two months) with which the book was written: a proofreader had to point out that the promised fate of one character had not been included and Stevenson had difficulty keeping early details in his head as he wrote the later portions. It falls rather uncomfortably into two clumsily coordinated parts with a break of some months in the narrative, and the generally episodic nature of the structure is not counterbalanced by an overriding narrative thrust. The broken-backed structure is particularly destructive of Stevenson's depiction of the relationship between Richard and Joanna. In the first part of the book Richard's attitude to Joanna is largely that of a boorishly ignorant youth's impatience with girlishness. In the later part, their story is that of knightly champion and threatened beloved: and to worship, serve, rescue, and eventually marry her becomes the driving impulse of his being – and of the narrative. Only, Stevenson shirks the business of exploring the process of his falling in love. But then, Stevenson is more concerned to depict his boy-hero developing into a 'bonnie fechter' (like Alan Breck) and a capable military commander (leading from the front, in a rather Errol Flynn kind of way). It is a very violent book but the reader, while scarcely surprised by the sheer volume of mortality (only to be expected in a novel about the Wars of the Roses), is likely to notice the almost total casualness with which Stevenson responds to the mayhem he is imagining in this book for young people. No B-movie medieval extravaganza could dispose of its spear-carriers with greater insouciance.

And if the language is bookish in the extreme, one is only too aware of the bookish nature of the novel's inspiration. Stevenson gets his 'facts' of the period from *The Paston Letters*, but when it comes to his treatment of this material his literary sources must have been many, varied, and fairly obvious. *Ivanhoe* and its many successors in Victorian historical fiction were inevitably influential, and Shakespeare's history plays scarcely less so. Beyond these, it would seem that another of Shakespeare's works, *As You Like It* once again, also helped colour the novel with its lightness, its sprightliness, its evocation of the greenwood and its device of the girl disguised as a boy. And mention of this romance reminds us of other romance works from Edmund Spenser and John Keats. ('The Eve of St Agnes' was surely in the background, with its perilous entrance into an enemy stronghold in search of a beloved lady, and its final vision of a solitary monk's demise.) Scott is clearly a general influence and inspiration (one is aware of novels other than *Ivanhoe* – *Waverley*, for example, and *Old Mortality* – playing their part, however briefly, in Stevenson's string of narrative inventions), though Stevenson has little interest in Scott's great theme of historical process, nor does he write historical fiction to demonstrate progress as Scott does. For Stevenson, the historical setting is the equivalent of *Treasure Island*'s geographical distance: it provides a playground where romantic adventure finds a natural home, where swords can clash and landscape can be roamed over. One wonders, too, if another Scottish novelist of Scott's generation, James Hogg, might be lurking somewhere in the background: his *The Three Perils of Man* (1822) has a wily Border chieftain holding back and calculating before deciding whether or not to join in the latest cross-border conflict in something of the same manner as Sir Daniel Brackley here, and it also features pretty heroines in boyish disguise. And as

Frank McLynn points out,[27] one could argue that it is in *The Black Arrow* that Stevenson introduces the motif of the double into his fiction, the Romantic stereotype which Hogg had so memorably employed. 'Richard' is the name of both the central character and also of the most memorable one: Crookback, as McLynn says, is Richard Shelton's *alter ego*.

The fact that so many readers, eminent and otherwise, of Stevenson's day and our own, have felt that *The Black Arrow* is notably inferior to the best of Stevenson's works does not mean, however, that it can be completely dismissed. It has its share of Stevensonian interest and strengths. Along with all the boyish immaturity (whether it arises from the book's intended audience of young people, or from a lingering boyishness in Stevenson's own creative personality) there is also evidence of a sufficiently mature outlook on life, and of what we can now see as a typically Stevensonian fascination with the complexities of morality and of human psychology. But the reader must persevere to the end to reach this level of insight. McLynn's observation about Crookback being Dick's double or *alter ego* provides the clue: it is when Dick is finally fully caught up in England's warring struggle which has hitherto provided merely the context for his own private adventures that he is confronted with the moral realities involved in the life of derring-do. If Stevenson shirks Scott's always careful (and partially judgemental) analyses of the differences and issues between his various warring forces, he makes (arguably) an alternative point – that there is nothing to choose between the parties of York and Lancaster – and conveys the futility of the violence of the age, a futility which his hero finally realizes as he opts for private, domestic bliss. And along the way, Dick receives some important moral shocks. In particular, as he makes his escape from the house of his enemies, he encounters the old ship-captain Arblaster, whose vessel he had hijacked then wrecked in his earlier rescue attempt, lamenting his loss. This brings home to Dick the disastrous cost to another entailed in his own private obsession with Joanna. He is further dismayed once he throws in his lot with Richard Crookback's Yorkists: the misshapen prince entrusts him with a crucial command (a trust which Dick amply justifies), but his trust (as Dick discovers) does not prevent him making provision for Dick's instant assassination should his loyalty prove in any way suspect: ' "Go, Dutton, and that right speedily," he added. "Follow that lad. If ye find him faithful, ye answer for his safety, a head for a head. Woe unto you, if ye return without him! But if he be faithless – or, for one instant, ye misdoubt him – stab him from behind." ' (*BA* 219) Crookback is the embodiment of stark alternatives, a leader who inspires his men totally but who is yet known for the ruthlessness with which he punishes any failure. Stevenson is clearly responding to Shakespeare's Richard III, so full of the 'hellish energy' he wrote about to Colvin. As a character, Crookback is the presiding spirit of the latter part of the book, focusing the conflicting glory and terror which make up the world of warfare and political rivalry – the world of 'history', we might say, as portrayed somewhat simply in this boyish romance. Our hero Dick has been able to succeed and thrive in that world, but as he does so he discovers another part of himself, little suspected at the outset. Like Scott's Edward Waverley, he reaches the point where he turns his back on military adventures and the fate of nations, retiring into domestic security and connubial bliss. Where Waverley's retreat, however, had led him to the point where 'he felt himself entitled to say firmly, though perhaps with a sigh, that the romance of his life was ended, and that its real history had now commenced', Dick Sheldon has to make no such transition from romance to realism.[28] Indeed, he remains in the realm of romance, the greenwood spirit of *As You Like It* prevailing: 'Thenceforth the dust and blood of that unruly epoch passed them by. They dwelt apart from alarms in the green forest where their love began.' (*BA* 265) It is one of the signs of the greater success of *Treasure Island* that Jim's corresponding rejection of the world of romance adventure feels a serious and living choice, compared to this storybook conclusion – especially as the greenwood, throughout the tale, has been the scene of multifarious threats and adventures, offering no promises of security.

This final oversimplification is a betrayal of the attempts at realism and historical accuracy throughout the book – evidence of Stevenson's sense of responsibility as a serious writer. But that there has been tension between his devotion to (on the one hand) psychological and historical truth and (on the other) romance narrative is suggested by the several occasions where he adds a footnote to indicate how he has deviated from what he knows to be the facts of history. And throughout, there have been strong indications of his consciousness of the real world of human beings even as he has spun his tale of juvenile romance: characters such as Bennet Hatch (a rough soldier prominent on the side of the villainous Sir Daniel Brackley but with a heart of gold and sympathetic to the young hero) or Lawless (an outlaw not to be trusted, as he himself admits, yet faithful to Dick and destined to die a friar) embody (as does Crookback) the duality which is the basis of so much of Stevenson's mature understanding of human life and behaviour. Amidst all the greenwood escapism and the swashbuckling energy, we can glimpse elements and ideas which form integral parts of Stevenson's best works: even now, readers are likely to respond differently to this somewhat unstable mixture, either regretting that so much of the best is wrapped up in a weak whole, or warming to the book's imperfections while reassured by its Stevensonian strengths.

3

'So easily the master of us all'

Edmund Gosse, writing to the author regarding the newly published *Prince Otto* (22 November 1885; Maixner 188–90), thus enthuses about what he regarded as the best aspects of that ambitious new work, and sums up much of the feeling with which London literary circles regarded Stevenson by the mid-1880s. Gosse and the others, particularly Henley and Colvin, had become his intimate friends, and continued to see themselves as, in a sense, midwives to his ever-emerging talent. This comfortable situation, however, had been made considerably less easy with Stevenson's marriage with Fanny Osbourne, who regarded herself as also something of a writer and critic, and whose influence on her new husband seldom coincided with theirs.

Considered geographically, the Stevenson marriage fell into three main phases: an attempt to live in France, a return to Britain which soon saw them settled in Bournemouth, then the journey west across the Atlantic which took them first to New York State, then to the South Seas and Samoa. Readers and critics the world over would probably now regard the supreme highlight of the Bournemouth years to be the writing of *Jekyll and Hyde*, of all Stevenson's many publications the one which has had both the widest and deepest impact on the modern consciousness. Only a little less universally appreciated, and usually more highly rated as an artistic achievement, was *Kidnapped*, the work, one could argue, which most perfectly satisfies the whole gamut of Stevenson's audiences, from children to literary critics. Taken along with *Treasure Island*, these three works constitute the core of Stevenson's place – a secure place – in the continuing awareness and esteem of posterity. Other works may run them close: clearly *The Master of*

Ballantrae is most memorable, the fictions about the South Seas are rightly argued for as major and distinctive achievements which ought to be more widely known and appreciated, and (perhaps by Scottish readers in particular) the unfinished *Weir of Hermiston* has been accorded a classic status partly based on what it contains, and partly on the drama and tragedy of its stark incompleteness.

In addition, however, to the two great products of his time in Bournemouth, the central point in Stevenson's brief career, there are various other works which are not only fascinating in themselves but which serve to complicate and enrich our sense of the diversity of his writing.

'MARKHEIM' (WRITTEN 1884)

'What makes a story true? Markheim is true; Olalla false; and I don't know why, nor did I feel it while I worked at them; indeed I had more inspiration with Olalla, as the style shows' (Maixner 250). Thus Stevenson in a letter to Colvin of January 1887, just before the two stories were re-printed in *The Merry Men and Other Tales and Fables*. 'Markheim' had been the earlier of the two; 'Olalla' was written immediately after *Jekyll and Hyde* in 1885 and the two short stories made their first appearances in the Christmas numbers of different periodicals in that year. Stevenson's comment, the proximity of their dates, and also their proximity to *Jekyll and Hyde* all constitute superficial reasons for linking them, but perhaps the principal reason for doing so is that (like the infinitely better known story they straddle) they both show Stevenson treating, with greater seriousness and focus than ever, the problem of the capacity for evil in all of us. In their settings and basic inspirations the two are quite different, but each envisages a seemingly inescapable strand of evil at the centre of its main characters. The tale, in each case, is about how one faces up to this dimension of our humanity, and what one does in response. The question, raised by Stevenson, as to which story is 'true' (that is, I take it, which story is the more imaginatively successful — which 'rings true', in other words) is perhaps less important than the way in which he works out, morally, his theme. Nevertheless, 'Markheim' is likely to strike one as the more haunting and gripping of the two; 'Olalla' seems somewhat creaky in comparison. Yet several recent commentators have shown a willingness to engage seriously with 'Olalla', and it is not to be denied that it demands consideration as a substantial step in Stevenson's unfolding creative journey. On the other hand, 'Markheim' is particularly distinguished by the confident detailing of its writing, as well as having an especial significance in that it marks the first wholly clear use which Stevenson made of the idea of the second self, or double – more clear, surely, than in *The Black Arrow*?

The issue of the relationship between 'Markheim' and Dostoevsky's *Crime and Punishment* (first published in 1866) is intriguing but not, finally, of overriding importance. Stevenson had certainly not read the English translation of Dostoevsky's novel when he wrote 'Markheim', as it was not published until 1886. We know that Stevenson received a copy of a French translation from his new friend Henry James during 1885 and this is the first contact with the novel which he is known to have had. As Claire Harman suggests, however, it is possible that Stevenson had encountered a French copy prior to this – before, that is, the writing of 'Markheim' in 1884 – but, from this point onwards, conjecture reigns.[1] The superficial resemblance of the two, in terms of their fictional starting-points, is undeniable: in each, a young man murders a sleazy pawnbroker, having persuaded himself that this is morally justifiable. Dostoevsky, of course, locates this in a long and complex novel whereas Stevenson merely focuses his short story on the minutes following the deed. And where the Russian murderer, trapped at the murder scene, follows up the first murder with a second (the pawnbroker's sister), Stevenson's story ends at the point at which Markheim decides not to slay the pawnbroker's returning servant-girl but to hand himself in to the police instead. The Scottish tale is all about Markheim's recognition and acceptance of the evil side of his being.

The means by which he reaches that point, which is a kind of salvation, is the strange figure who appears in the locked shop – the murder scene – and tempts him to escape the consequences of his violent act. Unlike Edward Hyde, soon to be released into the literary world, and unlike Olalla's vampire-like mother who embodies the degeneration of her Spanish family, this figure commits no violence. Instead, the new arrival merely offers complicity in the act of robbery and advises further murder as the only means of escaping the noose. But when Markheim rejects this way out and, insisting that he hates evil despite his actions, sends the maid for the police, this figure (variously referred to as 'the visitor', 'the other', 'the creature', 'the visitant') exhibits pleasure. It is true that this pleasure might be interpreted as the pleasure of a devil who has ensnared another soul, as Markheim hastens to a suicidal death by surrendering. But Stevenson's language suggests, rather, that the being is an emissary from the other side of the tracks and that it is in some sense heaven's work that he has been doing, rather than hell's. Perhaps the argumentative and tempting creature is not so much a devil as a devil's advocate? 'The features of the visitor began to undergo a wonderful and lovely change: they brightened and softened with a tender triumph; and, even as they brightened, faded and dislimned. But Markheim did not pause to watch or understand the transformation.' (VII, M. 118) We, however, are clearly invited to pause and understand. Surely the implication is that Markheim, in sparing the maid and accepting the fatal consequences of his action, has made the right choice – is in some sense saved, rather than finally falling into the devil's clutches?

The issue with which the story is concerned is surely indicated by the strange exchange at the outset, when the dealer offers a looking-glass as a possible present for the lady for whom Markheim claims he needs a last-minute Christmas gift. Markheim's reaction surprises both the dealer and the reader:

'A glass,' he said hoarsely, and then paused, and repeated it more clearly. 'A glass? For Christmas? Surely not?'

'And why not?' cried the dealer. 'Why not a glass?'

Markheim was looking upon him with an indefinable expression. 'You ask me why not?' he said. 'Why, look here – look in it – look at yourself! Do you like to see it? No! nor I – nor any man.' (M. 100–1)

The story is about our refusal to confront the facts of our nature, facts which include (as we discover while Markheim grapples with the arguments of his strange visitor) the self-comforting tendency to believe that, whatever foul acts we may commit (such as brutally killing a pathetic pawnbroker), we are no slaves to evil but creatures of a fundamental goodness. Our moral composition, thinks Markheim as he recoils in horror from the insinuations of (as he believes) the devil, is undefiled by whatever crimes or evils we commit under the pressure of the world's circumstances.

> 'And you would judge me by my acts! But can you not look within? Can you not understand that evil is hateful to me? Can you not see within me the clear writing of conscience, never blurred by any wilful sophistry, although too often disregarded? Can you not read me for a thing that surely must be common as humanity – the unwilling sinner?' (M. 113)

Is there, here, a distant echo – even, perhaps, a witty reversal – of that cherished doctrine of Scottish Evangelical Calvinism, that salvation is through Faith, not Works? Certainly, the 'visitant' apparently cares little for the crime but everything for the criminal: he has no interest in Markheim's claims to an essential purity.

> Evil, for which I live, consists not in action but in character. The bad man is dear to me; not the bad act, whose fruits, if we could follow them far enough down the hurtling cataract of the ages, might yet be found more blessed than those of the rarest virtues. And it is not because you have killed a dealer, but because you are Markheim, that I offered to forward your escape. (M. 115)

Note, however, the ambiguity of these words: at first glance they may seem to be those of a devil with a sinner just within his grasp. Equally, though, they could be those of an angel trying to save that same sinner – even that 'evil, for which I live' might bear the less obvious construction. We are naturally inclined to assume that any fictional 'double', designed by an author to seem part-supernatural and part-psychological, is meant to be a destructive, devilish force: we probably have Stevenson's own Edward Hyde and, possibly, Hogg's Gil-Martin to thank for that tendency. But here the arrival of the unexpected being follows, rather than precedes, murder. Consequently, a plausible initial stab at an interpretation of Markheim's creature might be 'conscience', rather. However, I agree with Claire Harman that we are here confronted with a final ambiguity of interpretation, and that this ambiguity is one of the story's strengths.

The ambiguity surrounding the strange creature, therefore, concerns both the nature of its being (psychological or super-natural or both?) and its moral orientation. But these ambi-guities flow with great inevitability from that other aspect of the story's mastery, namely the depiction of Markheim's sensations and state of mind between the murder and the creature's arrival. Even at a first encounter with the story, the vivid quality of the detail, and the illusion of psychological probability as Markheim finds himself alone with the corpse in the seconds after his sudden spasm of violence is likely to strike the reader as masterly. In particular, the reader is held by the pages which lie between the slaying itself and the arrival of the stranger, a passage in which very little outwardly happens but which occupies almost half the story's length (a clutch of clocks strike three; someone knocks at the shop door but goes away again; Markheim takes the shop keys from the corpse and moves from the shop into the dwelling behind it and then up to the first floor). The section is devoted to the observations, feelings, and thoughts of the central character as he finds himself, nerves and senses straining, in this extreme situation. From the start, Markheim's imagination (and Stevenson's verbal dexterity) animates the slightest things – the clocks, for example ('time had some score of small voices in that shop' (M. 102)) – and makes him fear the most ordinary sounds from outside. The room, illuminated by a single flickering candle, pulses with life – the descriptions suggesting, in part, the sheer vividness of Markheim's alertness to his surroundings but also, to some extent, the possibility of incipient madness or hallucination. His imagination turns the most ordinary things to a threat: the sounds in the still house, the life in the street outside, the dwellers in the houses in the immediate neighbourhood. 'But he was now so pulled about by different alarms that, while one portion of his mind was still alert and cunning, another trembled on the brink of lunacy.' (M. 105) And unreason builds to its perhaps inevitable climax: he knows he is alone in the house, yet he also fears and suspects that he is not alone. And it is from this context, of vividly depicted apprehension, hyper-sensitivity, and (eventually) unreason that the visitor emerges, its nature and status compromised from the start by the psychological point Markheim has reached.

And it is because the visitor appears to be the product of this intensely psychological context that we must interpret it mainly in psychological, rather than allegorical or supernatural, terms. It is an aspect of Markheim's self, let loose by the extraordinary strain he is now under. It is a hidden self, a double. While the 'visitant' does not exactly resemble Markheim (as in traditional stories of *doppelgängers*, or as in the case of Hogg's Robert Wringhim), there is the hint of a resemblance. Markheim is being forced to contemplate himself at last. Traditionally, also, the sight of one's *doppelgänger* foreshadows one's death, and this, too, is part of Stevenson's story. But whereas in *doppelgänger* lore, it would seem that the figure is essentially a supernatural one, we can perhaps best sum up what Stevenson is doing here by saying that he is filling the supernatural outline with a content of psychological possibility.

The latter part of the story is a static debate between the two figures, which is less of a disappointment to the thrill-seeking reader than it might have been. By the end of the tale, Markheim has honestly looked at himself and his deed, spared the maid and accepted the fatal consequences of his actions – accepted his evil, in fact. Stevenson tells here a tale of our capacity for evil, an evil not balanced by an equal tendency towards good although there is an apparent virtue in recognizing and accepting our fallen nature. Stevenson's universe may contain the devil, but it contains no simple deity of opposing goodness.

THE DYNAMITER (WRITTEN 1884–5)

Stevenson is now principally thought of as a tale-teller of islands, of Scotland, and of history. As *New Arabian Nights* is now largely forgotten by the common reader, he is not immediately remembered as a chronicler of Victorian London – until *Jekyll and Hyde* is recalled. The year before that key work appeared, however, he returned to his own already Arab-tinged London, with another Arabian night, *The Dynamiter* (1885). It was as if he needed to insist that Stevensonian romance could be drawn even from the prosaic reality of ordinary English life. The opening sentence articulates, as forcefully as before, everyday

London's potential as the generator of romantic narrative: 'In the city of encounters, the Bagdad of the West, and, to be more precise, on the broad northern pavement of Leicester Square, two young men of five- or six-and-twenty met after years of separation.' (III, *D.* 5) And the actuality of London's West End is underlined, a few moments later, when the pair take themselves off, fully in accordance with geographical probability, to 'a quiet establishment in Rupert Street, Soho'. This is the 'Bohemian Cigar Divan, by T. Godall' – in other words, a tobacconist's shop and smoking lounge (*D.* 5). Mundane Victorian reality and escapism thus continue intertwined: cigar divans were commonplace enough, but their function was escapist – male boltholes offering freedom simultaneously from work and domesticity. Stevenson was unlikely to be unaware of the term's fusing of commonplace Western city-life with the exoticism of the East. And the alert among *The Dynamiter*'s first readers may not have been surprised by the apparent ordinariness of the proprietor's name, remembering that 'T. Godall' had been Prince Florizel of Bohemia during an earlier 'night'.

In real life, London had recently seen incidents which had torn apart the familiarity of everyday normality: Irish and Irish-American Fenian terrorists had been conducting a bombing campaign since 1883, which had resulted in casualties amongst innocent bystanders and the bombers alike, as well as the highly effective destruction of property and infrastructure. This is the starting-point for Stevenson's book, avowedly written in collaboration once more with his wife Fanny. As so often in Stevenson's collaborations, it is unclear where his contribution begins and ends, but the disconcerting results have led many commentators to suspect Fanny's extensive involvement – which may reflect a continuing prejudice against her.

The jointly signed dedicatory note points to the confusion of attitudes and modes which make the book so puzzling in its effect: it acknowledges that the subject is crime, but the authors claim that mere criminality should not be written about seriously: 'it were a waste of ink to do so in a serious spirit'. Seriousness, they insist, is owed to 'acts of a more mingled strain, where crime preserves some features of nobility, and where reason and humanity can still relish the temptation' (*D.* xv). Crime can also give rise to nobility in others, such as Messrs

Cole and Cox, two police officers injured by a bomb at the House of Commons, to whom the book is dedicated. Fenian murderousness, however, evokes no respect whatsoever in the two authors, with the result that their fictional treatment of Irish plotters is startlingly comic and demeaning, and completely lacking in any attempt to comprehend their motivation. It is the role of the book's female love-interest, Clara Luxmore, to be attracted to the apparent nobility of their cause, only to eventually grow out of this foolish immaturity. The bombers themselves, in the persons of the bomb-maker Zero and his agent McGuire, are hapless failures at their own game, ineptly posturing bunglers. However, as Michael Burroughs has recently made clear, the real-life Fenian bombers shared some of the bungling black comedy of the Stevenson inventions: bombs would fail to ignite, or would go off prematurely.[2] Nevertheless, the Stevensons were writing towards the end of a series of Fenian bombing campaigns on the mainland of Britain which had begun in the later 1860s (soon after the end – not coincidentally – of the American Civil War) and which lasted for twenty years.

G. K. Chesterton put his finger on an obvious flaw in the book with his comment: 'It is really impossible to use a story in which everything is ridiculous to prove that certain particular Fenians or anarchist agitators are ridiculous. Nor indeed is it tenable that men who risk their lives to commit such crimes are quite so ridiculous as that.'[3]

Another difficulty arises from the book's structure. Where *New Arabian Nights* had been a daisy-chain of tales, their interconnectedness gradually being revealed (to the reader's gently surprised delight) to suggest a strange and romantic reality behind life's haphazardness, *The Dynamiter* attempts to develop and elaborate this method by embedding its constituent tales (equally as various as those of *New Arabian Nights*) in the world of the Fenian plotters. Furthermore, this world is itself variously entered by each of the three young men with whom the book starts. Stevenson's opening move is to contrive that Challoner, Somerset, and Desborough agree to open themselves to whatever adventure chance may bring them. In each case chance entangles them with the central figures of the Fenian plot – Clara, or Zero, or both – and each adventure becomes (as in 'The Rime of the Ancient Mariner') an encounter with a tale of another adventure. The satirical treatment of terrorism becomes the frame story for another collection of Stevensonian tall tales and the whole is designed, it would appear, to overwhelm the reader in the fictiveness of fiction. Which is all very well, except that the supposedly despicable Fenians have to be listened to, and so they become somewhat less despicable: they have the power to fascinate and entertain (both Stevenson's readers as well as their fictional auditors) and in Clara they include a figure of easy appeal and ready forgiveness. Some of the tales are apparently 'true' within the fiction (for example, Mrs Luxmore's weird adventure with Florizel and the assassin) while others are most elaborate whoppers (particularly, Clara's tales of Mormon oppression and the escape from Cuba). The book aims to be a bewildering kaleidoscope of narratives, the sense of confusion only heightened by the tenuousness between the tales told and the reasons for their telling: Clara, for example, concocts the whole elaborate tale of Mormon awfulness to explain to Challoner why she had to escape from the exploding house; Mrs Luxmore's story of Florizel and the assassin contributes only an explanation of why Somerset is being offered the house for nothing; and so on.

Clara, of course, turns out to be a regular Scheherazade and, as in the case of her Arabian predecessor, her seemingly infinite capacity to generate tales is fused with a measure of noble personal heroism. Like Maud Gonne a generation later, she combines youth, beauty, political idealism, and a willingness to use violence. She also possesses the supposedly endearing ability to twist young male strangers round her little finger, and to persuade them to undertake blind errands to distant parts of the United Kingdom. She tells two tales (complete lies, of course) each projecting herself as a vulnerable heroine and inevitably influencing our response to her: each one is designed to evoke fascination, respect for a survivor, and sheer pity in both her fictional auditors and her real-life readers. In the first she invents for herself origins in the Utah of American Mormonism, here portrayed as a sinister, oppressive, and all-pervasive cult apparently driven by the utterly ruthless greed of its leaders. Grierson, the particular Mormon with whom she has to deal, is further particularized by being a mad scientist whose aim is the discovery of a potion which will transform the elderly into their own younger selves. His purpose in striving for this is not merely the general human wish to escape the penalty of advancing years but the desire, more particularly, to be a physically fit husband able to fully possess a young wife. Problems with obtaining a sufficiently pure drug for the creation of the elixir results, she claims, in the explosion which Challoner witnesses. Her second invented autobiography, told this time to Desborough, sees her as the illegitimate daughter of a Cuban plantation owner. Her father, she says, had failed to have her status legitimized so that, legally, she is still part of the property being claimed by his creditors when he suddenly dies. Her escape involves buried treasure, a trek through a jungle (so disease-ridden that to enter it is death to most whites), the witnessing of a barbaric voodoo (or, as Stevenson has it, hoodoo) ceremony, and an escape to England where her slave-status is no longer relevant.

These tales exist in the book primarily for their own sake, of course: they are instances of Stevenson's (and Fanny's) concept of adventure fiction. They nevertheless have some interaction with their teller: they associate her (in the minds of both her fictional auditors and real-life readers) with hardihood, with the image of beauty oppressed, and with a hinterland of the utmost fascination and unpredictability. That is the idea, anyway. A brief précis of each of the tales (such as I have just given) is almost cruel in its suggestion of how much tosh they are, but there is an intensity in the telling which goes a long way to persuading the reader (as well as the tales' fictional auditors, although Challoner, to his credit, immediately suspects the tale he hears to be untrue). After all, both *Treasure Island* and *Jekyll and Hyde* also would seem so much tosh when summarized as briefly as this. Nevertheless, there is a hit-or-miss quality to these early tales of Stevenson: they may all be peculiarly Stevensonian, but they do not all rise to the effectiveness of 'The Suicide Club'. And although, at one level, their purpose is to contribute to a gallimaufry of fictions with the prime aim of constantly surprising the reader and demonstrating the inexhaustible fecundity of the writer's imagination, at another level they do interact with the frame story's concern with terrorism. In each case, Clara's fictional *alter ego* encounters intolerable oppression and shows courage in resisting it. And her tales both envisage the presence, in London, of secret, destructive organizations, somewhat like the Fenian one of which she is actually part. She is thus able to make the transition (in our estimation) from dangerous threat to rescue-worthy victim.

The other feature one notices about both these tales is the sexuality which comes surprisingly close to the surface in each. It goes beyond the broad-brush beauty-in-distress sex-appeal of a feisty heroine. In 'Story of the Destroying Angel', the desire of Grierson to be fully sexually potent once more (as well as simply younger and healthier) is clear, as is the sexual charge which makes 'Asenath' (Clara's Mormonized name for herself in the story) palpitate with expectation as her imposed husband draws near. And in 'Story of the Fair Cuban' there is (for its day) a surprisingly explicit episode as the fair Cuban encounters the 'hoodoo' jungle ceremony: it is presided over by 'a tall negro, entirely nude' and by the witch Madam Mendizabal 'naked also' (D. 194). Mendizabal's plea to her spirits is doubly interesting: 'I grow old, I grow hideous; I am known, I am hunted for my life: let thy servant then lay by this outworn body; let thy chief priestess turn again to the blossom of her days, and be a girl once more, and the desired of all men, even as in the past.' (D. 196) Like Grierson, she desires a miraculous return to youth, for its sexual advantages. But one also notices that her desire for a miraculous change of appearance also springs from a desire to escape her current identity and to avoid being 'hunted' for the evil she has done. As with Grierson's potion, and its impurity, one senses a future containing Jekyll and Hyde.

Clara is destined to renounce her violent idealism and to be granted a safe marriage: we last glimpse her being overheard in the cigar divan spinning some other yarn. Somerset and Desborough are 'hanging on her words with extraordinary interest' but, strikingly, Challoner had taken himself off 'from the detested neighbourhood of the enchantress' (D. 243). It is as if Stevenson were acknowledging that not all readers/hearers are going to be seduced by the amoral appeal of a well-told tale: Challoner is moralist enough to be unforgiving of the danger and humiliation he had suffered at her hands. For him, the real world has stronger claims than the enchantments of romance and heroic chivalry: the loss of his 'last good trousers and his last presentable coat' (*D.* 78) and the indignity of his Glasgow disguise have been too much.

But the figure who brings the conflict of the everyday and romance into sharpest focus is Zero, the dynamiter himself. He focuses the strange contradictions in the book – an awful reality in the real contemporary world (the Fenian bombing campaign) treated with levity, as a whimsical, decorative entertainment, and in such a way that the destructive reality of the campaign is constantly being blinked at and transformed into the excuse for a display of merely fictional inventiveness. Zero, his creativity producing not stories but one 'infernal machine' after another, sees himself as an artist rather than a political activist. His goal is the perfectly engineered time-bomb and he pursues it, as it were, for its own sake. He longs for success, not with a view to effecting political change but, rather, to preserve and enhance his reputation in the terrorist community. That he constantly fails to produce a workable bomb, and that he is eventually the only victim of his devices, makes him a comic figure who sits at the heart of all that is strange and unexpected about the work. Despite his activities, there is nothing sinister or threatening about this character's personality – or, at least, Zero himself does not think there is. He sees himself as a charming, sensitive, creative person who longs for, and deserves, sympathetic and appreciative company. Stevenson derives much comedy, in the latter pages of the book, from Zero's hurt responses to Somerset's growing detestation of the man with whom he finds himself entangled. Fenian goals are not being pursued for political ends, but for creative and artistic ones, it would seem. Deaglán Ó'Donghaile, in his excellent account of Stevenson's contribution to the literature of terrorism which emerged in the 1880s, is particularly strong in bringing out the idea of terrorism as an aesthetic endeavour.[4] Both Clara and Zero are versions of the artist: it is possible to interpret the book as an exploration of the place of art in the world. Clara's presence in the book suggests that the fecundity of artistic inspiration is endlessly appealing, whatever its context in a real-life situation; Zero suggests that it is possible to create art, and respond to it, with none of the moral expectations of the Victorians, in particular.

Instead, the vision of art he articulates offers creative effort and energy, and a striving to achieve a complex, finely judged end-product, as all the justification that is needed. Zero the artist sets his own goals and does not expect to be judged by them; for him, the final success of the design and its incarnation are everything. He owes moral responsibility to no one.

This is an attitude which may provoke in us either approval or outrage. Is Stevenson sanctioning this vision, or is he attacking (or at least satirizing) it? The nature of the book he has produced would appear to suggest the former: *The Dynamiter* is as far from being a heavily, and inescapably, moral expression as one can conceive and its subject matter seems to have been chosen with a view to making exactly that point. The treating of a terrorist campaign with levity, and without any clear condemnation, must have struck contemporary readers as being almost as shocking and perverse as it undoubtedly does today. Alan Sandison has discussed at length the unexpected thinking lying behind Stevenson's approach here and, in so doing, offers *The Dynamiter* as one of its author's most individual and glorious texts. In Sandison's eyes, Stevenson is offering art as pure entertainment – just as the ducking and diving of Clara's tales offers no apologia or explanation for terrorism. They simply stand alone, their ability to hold their readers' attention their sole justification.[5] But Sandison's view, eloquent, erudite, innovative, and passionate as it is, has not necessarily swept all before it: the reader's own encounter with the book itself is still liable to leave doubt, disquiet, and bafflement in the mind. Yet one has to say that it seems wrong that *The Dynamiter*, and its predecessor volume, should be now elbowed so far aside in the modern response to Stevenson. In its wit, its unfailing grace-fulness of style, and its prodigality of narrative invention, it expresses its author as fully as anything he ever wrote and one can at least partly understand Chesterton's fleeting temptation to see the two volumes of *New Arabian Nights* as Stevenson's greatest work, on the grounds that, of all his output, 'it is probably the most unique; there was nothing like it before, and, I think, nothing equal to it since'.[6]

If critics fall into different camps in their final assessment of *The Dynamiter*, they also fall into different camps over the question of how to respond to the shared authorship. Frank

McLynn, for example, in his 1993 biography which is, in one of its narrative strands, a sustained attack on Fanny Stevenson, has no difficulty in seeing all its weaknesses as simple evidence of Fanny's bumptious lack of talent.[7] Others, above all Sandison, almost completely ignore Fanny's undoubted presence in the work and treat it as coming from the hand of the master, pure and simple. Brief but sympathetic references to Fanny and her hand in *The Dynamiter*, however, are to be found in the discussions of the book by Stevenson's modern female biographers Jenni Calder and Claire Harman, while Robert Fraser also reminds us how it was Fanny who concocted the Mormon and Cuban tales as a way of entertaining and supporting Stevenson in one of his bouts of illness.[8] Both Calder and Harman are prepared to credit Stevenson's wife with a potential talent which her married circumstances stifled – a notion which McLynn would see as preposterous. Fanny is a divisive figure to this day.

'OLALLA' (WRITTEN 1885)

'Markheim' strikes one as an appropriate companion to *Jekyll and Hyde*, and 'Olalla' is another such. At first glance it is a very different sort of story, with its tale of a British officer convalescing in the household of a strange Spanish family (it is presumably to be understood as taking place during the Peninsular War). That this is an ancient family which has in some sense degenerated into madness through generations of isolation is gently stressed from the outset, and sudden outbreaks of bestial behaviour – the son savagely maltreats a squirrel, and the mother, vampire-like, attacks the officer after he cuts his wrist badly – gradually reveal the crisis which afflicts the current family members. Eventually, the officer (who remains unnamed) encounters the daughter of the household. Far from being (as he had suspected) the mad source of the wild nocturnal cries he had been hearing, she turns out to be by far the most normal of the three and, furthermore, she is stunningly beautiful. It is love at first sight:

> I went very lightly across the court and up the marble staircase. My foot was on the topmost round, when a door opened, and I found

myself face to face with Olalla. Surprise transfixed me; her loveliness struck to my heart; she glowed in the deep shadow of the gallery, a gem of colour; her eyes took hold upon mine and clung there, and bound us together like the joining of hands; and the moments we thus stood face to face, drinking each other in, were sacramental and the wedding of souls. (VII, O. 163–4)

The story prompts Stevenson to one of his occasional attempts to create a sexual woman:

She was dressed with something of her mother's coquetry, and love of positive colour. Her robe ... clung about her with a cunning grace. After the fashion of that country, besides, her bodice stood open in the middle, in a long slit, and here, in spite of the poverty of the house, a gold coin, hanging by a ribbon, lay on her brown bosom. (O. 166)

The officer is predictably infatuated and longs to have her as his wife; she too, we are to understand, is attracted to him. But she is all too aware of her family curse: each succeeding generation presents an ever-deepening threat to all around them, and the local peasantry would rise to murderous destruction if it became known that a yet further generation might be produced. Word of the love of the pair is beginning to circulate and they are consequently in danger. She refuses even to depart with him forever, accepting instead, with Christian resignation, her fate as the victim of what earlier generations have passed down to her: 'behold the face of the Man of Sorrows. We are all such as He was – the inheritors of sin; we must all bear and expiate a past which was not ours; there is in all of us – ay, even in me – a sparkle of the divine. Like Him, we must endure for a little while, until morning returns bringing peace.' (O. 186) Like Markheim, Olalla is forced to accept her own nature and the reality of her tainted being. And as the narrator contemplates her and the image of the suffering Christ on which she leans, he seems to be encouraging us to accept 'sad and noble truths', that 'pleasure is not an end, but an accident; that pain is the choice of the magnanimous; that it is best to suffer all things and do well'. (O. 187)

There is a portentous, willed piety in this conclusion, however, and a measure of sentimentality over a love affair which is thwarted by heredity: the ending seems to arise out of a different impulse from the Gothic mystery and threat which characterizes the bulk of the tale. So it is no surprise to read, at the end of Stevenson's essay 'A Chapter on Dreams', that most of the details of the main body of the story had come to him in a dream. Much of it was the work, he tells us, of 'The Brownies', the night-time subconscious workings of his own mind while asleep from which, he claims, much of his inspiration as a writer had its origin. *Jekyll and Hyde* is his other illustration of the gifts he had received from 'The Brownies': his brief account there supplements Fanny's famous tale of waking up her nightmare-gripped bed-mate and being upbraided for cutting short such an intense and creatively promising vision.[9]

Stevenson's little story nevertheless rests in comparative obscurity, overshadowed on either side by the two best-known examples of vampire literature in English from the later nineteenth century, Sheridan Le Fanu's *Carmilla* (1872) and Bram Stoker's *Dracula* (1897). Nor does one have to look far for other examples of vampires in literature from exactly the same period, such as George MacDonald's title-character in *Lilith* (1895). Literary vampires were available to writers in English, as it were, from the time of Coleridge's 'Christabel' (1816) and Polidori's *The Vampyre* (1819) onwards. Vampires and their Gothic hinterland are well-recognized elements of the Victorian literary scene. They are also, of course, great favourites in twentieth-century culture, not least in the present day. It would be foolish to claim that Stevenson's story had much to do with that, but Sara Wasson has written an interesting account of how Stevenson's conception of vampirism essentially differs from Stoker's and consequently does seem to foreshadow the way that the motif has been often handled in our own time.[10] Essentially, she points out, Stoker's vampirism involves being bitten, so that the condition spreads like a disease. Stevenson, however, imagines vampirism as a hereditary condition, passed down from the past, thereby trapping the individual in quite a different way. Vampirism is in our genes, as it were. Hilary J. Beattie also focuses on 'Olalla' in her brief but intensely psychoanalytical study of Stevenson's writing: it constitutes her main text for discussion, though she also relates it to *Jekyll and Hyde* and to *Weir of Hermiston* in particular.[11] Her account is particularly interesting for its survey of the literary influences to be detected in the story.

'Markheim' and 'Olalla', variable successes as they may be, confirm the idea that around this stage in his career Stevenson was engaging ever more closely with the depths of the personality, and with an exploration of human psychology. It is a fascination which would continue to mark, in various ways, the writings which he was yet to produce, including the important novel left at his death, *Weir of Hermiston*. Those later works would be as varied and unpredictable, however, as those he had already published. Stories seemed to come to him, more frequently than not, as unexpected inspirations and the result was his notable variety. An origin in dreams may go some way to explain this, just as his stress on the dream-work which he describes so elegantly in 'A Chapter on Dreams' may also explain why he can seem to be so modern. Dreams, after all, were (or were about to be) in the air, and not just in Vienna. And it was from this personal dream-source that he produced the tale which still seems most relevant today.

STRANGE CASE OF DR JEKYLL AND MR HYDE (WRITTEN 1885)

Strange Case of Dr Jekyll and Mr Hyde is the work of Stevenson's which has escaped, in the minds of readers and critics the world over, from the various niche categories which now enclose, and for many potential readers cordon off, his other major achievements. Perhaps *Treasure Island* runs it close in universal awareness, and is probably the other work which will still spring to the mind of most readers whenever Stevenson's name is mentioned. But *Treasure Island* has never ceased to be regarded as a book primarily for children, despite the pleasure an adult can find in it. Now, only *Jekyll and Hyde* (to abbreviate the title) best allows Stevenson to retain that reputation which he once had as a universally venerated classic author. It is currently the work which, for our generation at least, confirms his place in world literature: in recent histories of English literature, for example, it is usually to this little 'shilling shocker' that the modern literary historian turns first, and considers most extensively. As William B. Jones writes, *Jekyll and Hyde* is 'unquestionably the focal point of academic interest in the author's work.'[12]

To a critic like J. H. Millar in 1903, however, *Jekyll and Hyde* was merely 'a tolerable, but by no means an exceptional, specimen of its author's art'.[13] Millar could not have foreseen how the tale would transfer to the twentieth-century media of cinema and television, despite its near-instant theatrical incarnation in Thomas Russell Sullivan's 1887 stage version in Boston and New York. (The work's first transformation of all, however, must have been the brief spoof which appeared within weeks, in *Punch*, on 6 February 1886.) It was the cinematic versions, however, which enabled the tale to seep permanently into the consciousness of the English-speaking world. The inevitable simplifications necessary whenever a book is transferred to the screen have had the effect of highlighting, to an extraordinary extent, the narrative essence of the tale with its central imagery, the stark contrast between an appearance which is urbane and civilized, and one which is monstrous. And with this, we have grasped the notion that each of us is, morally and psychologically, a contradictory person and the site of astonishingly warring tendencies. Furthermore, the filmic distillation of Stevenson's tale provided the twentieth century, possessed in any case (thanks above all to Freud) of scientific assurance that each of us conceals hidden complexities, with both a memorable narrative embodiment of that proposition and (perhaps just as important) an equally memorable and handy phrase with which to grasp the phenomenon: 'Jekyll and Hyde'.

The simple balance of the phrase, however, tends to lead the popular expectation in too crude a direction: in common parlance, it has come to signify merely the opposite inclinations towards good and evil in each of us. *Chambers English Dictionary* defines the phrase in just those terms: 'the good side and the bad side of a human being'. Arnold Kemp's application of it to bigoted Scottish football supporters is typical: 'I have seen respectable men, sober in their habits, kind to their wives and children, solicitous of their pets, undergo a Jekyll-and-Hyde transformation at Ibrox or Parkhead. The civilised veneer is wiped from their faces and they become incoherent, babbling with hatred.'[14] Stevenson's original tale, however, offers a far more complicated, less clear-cut treatment of the two incarnations of the central character. Jekyll in particular is morally complex, and far from the allegory of goodness which the standard use of the phrase implies, while his denunciation of Hyde as 'pure evil' – a formula which launched the simplified vision of Hyde for successive generations of readers and viewers – gives voice to the panic he is experiencing at the terror-filled climax of his story rather than offering us a totally trustworthy interpretation of his other self. Hyde is also a somewhat more contradictory figure than the phrase implies. Indeed, one of the complicating aspects of the story is that we have our most complete account of Hyde from Jekyll himself rather than from any more detached character (let alone an omniscient narrator), and Jekyll's words, in 'Henry Jekyll's Full Statement of the Case', are steeped in self-justification and moral slipperiness from the beginning. Even at the end, when one might have expected last-minute honesty, he is still trying to distance himself from Hyde.

Does one refer to 'Jekyll' and to 'Hyde' as two characters, or as one? This is only one of the multiple ambiguities involved in the story. We do not even have a simple unchallengeable account of its writing. The 'official' account given in the biography of Stevenson by his cousin Graham Balfour – 'official' because the biography was written at the behest, and under the influence, of Stevenson's widow – gives her a pivotal role: she claimed to have criticized the first draft because it was (she said) a merely superficial tale which missed the opportunity for 'it was really an allegory'.[15] Stung by this criticism (we are told), Stevenson impulsively burned his first draft and quickly produced another which took his central character(s) much closer to embodying the obvious moral opposites. Jenni Calder accepted this account, but more recent critics reject it, doubting that Stevenson, even when writing in great haste in order to make some much needed cash, could have been a less penetrating critic than his wife.[16] The general outlines of the story's creation seem firm: its origin in a nightmare, the swiftness of the writing of both versions, the critical intervention of the wife, the burning of the first draft. What is disputed is the likely grounds for Fanny's criticism, and the notion that the second version which we now have is undoubtedly superior to the lost original despite Stevenson claiming, on first showing it to Fanny (as Nellie Sanchez recalled), that that had been 'the best thing he had ever done'.[17] McLynn suspects that Fanny was horrified by a new strain of openness about sex in the first draft, possibly fearing that this development would harm his image as a universally wholesome writer and, in particular, a writer associated with highly successful books for children. That sexuality lurks potently within the tale is assumed by latter-day critics and readers alike, despite the fact that there is no overt treatment of the topic in the story as we have it. There is little doubt that Stevenson was particularly conscious, as he wrote the story, of what he referred to in a letter to John Addington Symonds (early March 1886) as 'that damned old business of the war in the members'. Yet even here there is ambiguity. Here is the somewhat fuller quotation: 'Jekyll is a dreadful thing, I own; but the only thing I feel dreadful about is that damned old business of the war in the members. This time it came out; I hope it will stay in, in future.' (Mehew, 310) Does 'came out' and 'stay in' mean that sex had emerged for once as a constituent of this story whereas he hopes that future tales will manage to keep it under wraps – or does he here express regret that an original version was open about sexual behaviour but that this was expunged ('came out') in a maimed version given to the public? Whichever it may be, readings of our own day – inexhaustibly various as they are – approach *Jekyll and Hyde* as a tale which is steeped in an awareness of sex. Stevenson's most open account of this came in another letter, this time to John Paul Bocock (November 1887):

> Hyde was the younger of the two. He was not good looking however; and not, Great Gods! a mere voluptuary. There is no harm in a voluptuary; and none, with my hand on my heart and in the sight of God, none – no harm whatever – in what prurient fools call 'immorality.' The harm was in Jekyll, because he was a hypocrite – not because he was fond of women; he says so himself; but people are so filled full of folly and inverted lust, that they can think of nothing but sexuality. The Hypocrite let out the beast Hyde – who is no more sexual than another, but who is the essence of cruelty and malice, and selfishness and cowardice: and these are the diabolic in man – not this poor wish to have a woman, that they make such a cry about. I know, and I dare to say, you know as well as I, that bad and good, even to our human eyes, has no more connection with what is called dissipation than it has with flying kites. But the sexual field and the business field are perhaps the two best fitted for the

> display of cruelty and cowardice and selfishness. That is what people see; and these they confound. (Mehew 352)

This view of the matter, that the story is essentially about the need for honesty and the acceptance of aspects of ourselves which society may disapprove of, has become a modern orthodoxy, replacing the initial (and understandable) Victorian focus on the idea of a shocking duality in our nature. By 1886, the idea that we are dual (at the very least) was no longer a novelty, although the story hit home with its first readers, and finally consolidated Stevenson's reputation throughout the English-speaking world, because of the peculiar forcefulness of the tale he had devised to embody our doubleness. Many modern readings, however, focus less on Hyde and what he may 'stand for', or even on the insight that we are 'double'; they concentrate more on Jekyll and his society, and on his response to that society. Thus, Edwin Eigner builds on the notion that 'the harm was in Jekyll, because he was a hypocrite', while Sandison explores the hints regarding Jekyll's world, and the nature and behaviour of the apparently minor characters in the story, with great subtlety and ingenuity.[18]

Indeed, when one turns again to the story itself, it is striking how much emphasis there is on the reactions of others to Jekyll/ Hyde: the fantasy story of the unlikely scientific breakthrough and incredible physical transformation of Jekyll into Hyde is, in part at least, a way of expressing Stevenson's clear-eyed vision of respectable British society. Jekyll's special distinction becomes less a matter of astonishing (if disastrous and morally dubious) scientific achievement and more one of peculiar hypersensitivity to a world in which, it seems, reputation is all. Thus, as Sandison indicates, the early pages involving Utterson and Enfield serve not merely to introduce Hyde and his mysterious behaviour, as a first reading might suggest, but also raise questions about the mystery of Utterson and Enfield themselves. What is, and has been, their relationship? Why are two such different people attracted to each other's company? How loaded is the description of Enfield as 'the well-known man about town'?[19] We deduce that the pair are under constant observation by others and are the objects of speculation, just as Jekyll and Hyde soon will be – and it is open to us to speculate as well. The most powerful threat which Enfield can think of to induce Hyde to make financial restitution for his trampling of the child is the promise that 'we could and would make such a scandal out of this, as should make his name stink from one end of London to the other' (*JH* 7). For much of the story, while Utterson pieces together the fragments of insight he thinks he is gleaning regarding Jekyll's difficulties, his fear is primarily for his friend's reputation. And it is reputation which is the over-whelming issue in Jekyll's account, in the two long opening paragraphs of 'Henry Jekyll's Full Statement of the Case': in splitting 'Hyde' apart from himself, the scientist's goal had been an untarnished reputation for good works for the Jekyll the world perceives, and a reputation-free environment for the pleasures of his Hyde-self, pleasures which he describes, lightly and obscurely, as deriving merely from 'a certain impatient gaiety of disposition'(*JH* 52). (His confession may be labelled a 'full statement of the case', but even while spilling the beans, Jekyll cannot bring himself to spell them out.) Reputation, and a tendency to judge from appearances, permeates the world of the story, which is hardly surprising given that these men – Jekyll, Lanyon, Utterson, and their friends – inhabit an environment in which reputation is not only the dominant value but is also, it would appear, in a constant state of precariousness. Thus, Utterson's whole professional life involves him in dealing with, and trying to rescue, 'down-going men', victims of their own 'high pressure of spirits' (*JH* 5), (phrasing, once more, which implies a light-touch morality) so that pleasure and self-indulgence would appear to be what one must avoid if one is to have a cast-iron reputation, just as Utterson does and as Jekyll desires. A folly from one's past, in this world, is a constant threat, as is a misstep in the present. Even as he writes his final statement to the world, Jekyll cannot bring himself to indicate clearly what it was he had so shamefully got up to, an omission which has allowed a wealth of interpretations and suppositions by later readers.

And if the story avoids telling us about Jekyll/Hyde's favourite indulgences, it equally avoids telling us much about the Hyde-self which enjoys them. In most dramatic treatments of the tale, the clear revelation of Hyde as an object of horror is a natural climax, but Stevenson avoids giving us a description of him beyond informing us that he is young and small. This omission, obviously, is so as to allow each of us to imagine our own personal 'Hyde', but it also throws the focus onto those who encounter him. Our sense of Hyde as visually repellent, but only in some mysterious way, derives completely from the fact that that is how other characters perceive him. Enfield is typical: 'He is not easy to describe. There is something wrong with his appearance; something displeasing, something down-right detestable. I never saw a man I so disliked, and yet I scarce know why. He must be deformed somewhere; he gives a strong feeling of deformity, although I couldn't specify the point.' (*JH* 9) A double mystery, then, both as regards what Hyde looks like and also what he does. If Fanny was really motivated to induce her husband to turn his first draft into a resounding allegory, she was some way from success: Hyde is hidden from us to a large extent, and Jekyll, a fascinating mixture of creditable and culpable impulses, is too individual a case to be easily pinned down to a simple allegorical meaning. Stevenson's own judgement upon him, that he is a hypocrite, sums up much of what he represents. Despite the many sermons which were apparently delivered in 1886 in response to its appearance, the book cannot easily be claimed as a treatment of Good and Evil in any religious or philosophical context. Rather, it has to be seen as an exploration of our moral complexity, viewed purely in the contexts of our human, and particularly social, selves. The cheerfully unrealistic, romance nature of the tale should not trick us into attempting an emblematic reading.

We twice *see* Hyde being 'evil': when he treads on the child, and when he murders Carew. The latter case is necessary so that we are convinced that he is, after all, capable of performing an act so extreme that it is not to be ignored or forgiven under any moral scheme. It is also needed so as to create a situation in which 'being Hyde' becomes untenable just at the point when the action of the potion makes the Hyde state inescapable – hence the tragic end. The murder is not, it would appear, a typical act of the Hyde state: before the murder, all that we are told is that once Hyde is made the guise in which Jekyll indulges his 'undignified' pleasures, 'they soon began to turn towards the monstrous' and Jekyll is horrified by the 'depravity' of pleasures which could involve 'any degree of torture to another' (*JH* 57). Even here, however, the stress is not on the absolute awfulness of the depraved acts in themselves, but on the spirit of total selfishness, of complete indifference to the feelings and rights of another: 'his every act and thought centred on self' (*JH* 57). This, surely, is also the point of the incident with the child which, by its position at the outset, must be intended to indicate to us, however obscurely, what it is about Hyde which sets him apart from all others. What is horrific about Hyde here is his total lack of any instinct to avoid hurting this most vulnerable of fellow mortals: that is his essential monstrosity. And that too is the freedom, essentially, which Jekyll has found for himself in creating, or releasing, him: an unnatural state of obliviousness to the feelings and judgement of others is his extreme response to the otherwise all-enclosing environment of society's opinion which makes 'reputation' so central. Stevenson's own summary, in the letter to Bocock, of what is diabolical in us and (by implication) in Hyde, has everything to do with the way we interact with those around us: 'Hyde who is the essence of cruelty and malice, and selfishness and cowardice: and these are the diabolic in man – not this poor wish to have a woman, that they make such a cry about.' He is rejecting, here, the standard moral code of his time, steeped as it was in religious justification, in favour of a morality derived from the direct experience of living.

This reading of Hyde, however – that he is the epitome of selfishness, a being free from conscience, and inhumanly untouched by the opinion of others both because of his own nature and also because his ability to turn back into Jekyll makes meaningless any bad reputation he might acquire – does not cover everything which Stevenson says about him. When (in the 'full statement of the case') Jekyll touches upon the murder of Carew he refers both to Hyde's 'complete moral insensibility' but also to his 'insensate readiness to evil' and to a 'more furious propensity to ill' (*JH* 60). In part, Stevenson seems to be envisaging, after all, a creature with a positive urge to do harm, the malevolent, predatory Hyde of popular imagination, a diabolic incarnation of evil with a natural instinct to hurt others. This is essentially different from the way Jekyll claims to have envisaged the opposites which he might separate by means of his compound. In his account of his hopes for success, Jekyll talks simply of the 'unjust [going] his way, delivered from the aspirations and remorse of his more upright twin'(*JH* 53). This implies, merely, a fairly ordinary sinner released from the frowns and judgements of a puritanical associate. Is there not confusion here? At times, it seems to be the confusion of a Jekyll who, even at the end, cannot bring himself to fully confront what he has done; at other times, the confusion feels like Stevenson's.

What is Hyde, in relation to Jekyll? Is he an embodiment of a dimension of positive evil in each one of us, as Jekyll says: 'and Edward Hyde, alone in the ranks of mankind, was pure evil' (*JH* 55). Or is he essentially, and merely, a disguise – an embodiment of the pleasure-seeking side of Jekyll's nature which is released through the simple expedient of a radical change of appearance? Balfour's account of the first, destroyed, version baldly describes Hyde in it as a straightforward disguise for the sinning Jekyll.[20] On the other hand, the story sometimes describes the moments of transformation as involving not only a change of appearance, but an inner change as well, as when the potion is first swallowed.

> There was something strange in my sensations, something indescribably new and, from its very novelty, incredibly sweet. I felt younger, lighter, happier in body; within I was conscious of a heady recklessness, a current of disordered sensual images running like a mill race in my fancy, a solution of the bonds of obligation, an unknown but not an innocent freedom of the soul. I knew myself, at the first breath of this new life, to be more wicked, tenfold more wicked, sold a slave to my original evil; and the thought, in that moment, braced and delighted me like wine. (*JH* 54)

Similarly, when Jekyll takes the potion again, after a long period of abstinence, an inner transformation takes place once more: 'I was conscious, even when I took the draught, of a more unbridled, a more furious propensity to ill.'(*JH* 60) On the other hand, on at least one occasion, when he first transforms into Hyde spontaneously, Jekyll seems to retain his Jekyll-consciousness fully, and looks in horror at the Hyde-appearance he sees in the mirror. Vestiges of the story's original concept of a Hyde-disguise therefore remain, and there is a similar complexity, indeed confusion, in the way Jekyll refers to Hyde. Sometimes, Hyde is 'I' – after all, 'this, too, was myself' (*JH* 55); at other times, Hyde is very much 'he' as Jekyll attempts to disown him. The mixture across the story as a whole is embodied in the initial transformation just quoted: the feeling described is one of Hyde's sensations of freedom and wickedness, while at the same time we assume that it is also still Jekyll who is examining his feelings.

If there is confusion in all this, it is scarcely to be wondered at, and one must acknowledge that it has done little to impair the pleasure countless readers have taken in the tale. Stevenson's initial dream inspiration of a transformation produced by 'powders' seems simple enough, as does his sense of our double nature. However, when such a tale comes to be elaborated, the complexity of deciding whether to think of Jekyll and Hyde as one being or two is considerable, and it is worth recalling that Stevenson never hesitated to admit that it was written in extraordinary haste, to make some money. Yet the inspiration was clearly sound in its reflection of something true which modern readers have found to be fascinating and important, and the complexity both of the concept and of the finished piece of writing has engaged readers and critics to a greater extent than any other of Stevenson's works.

At first glance, *Strange Tale of Dr Jekyll and Mr Hyde* appears to be another version of the Faust myth: an exceptionally gifted mortal isolates himself from the rest of mankind by achieving knowledge and a goal which elevates him above the rest of us, but finds that he has crossed a line and taken, as it turns out, a disastrous step. In nineteenth-century fiction, Stevenson's tale seems to be in the immediate company of *Frankenstein*, *The Private Memoirs and Confessions of a Justified Sinner*, and *The Picture of Dorian Gray*. In other words, we might be forgiven for assuming, as so many first readers no doubt did, that Stevenson's point has everything to do with Jekyll and his foolish and immoral application of his scientific genius. But it is possible to regard this (by 1885) hackneyed tale and lesson as merely the element from which emerges the vision of the world with which the story is really concerned, namely the very attempt itself (which we are making in every moment of our conscious lives) to know each other, although that knowledge is always radically unreachable. Jekyll's ability to turn into Hyde, and vice versa, allegorizes not just the complexity and contra-dictoriness within each of us but (even more radically) the fact that our innermost reality can never be guessed or grasped by anyone else except, possibly, through an act of our own total self-revelation. The structure of the story, after all, is provided by Utterson's prolonged attempt to find out the truth about his friend Jekyll, little suspecting that that is as unique as it turns out to be.

The truth of William B. Jones's comment above, however, is testimony to the extraordinary qualities of the tale, even in the context of Stevenson's output. No other work of his comes near it in generating critical and interpretative interest – a testimony both to its psychological resonances and to its endless ambiguities. There are several favoured lines of approach. The suspicion that the tale strongly reflects the homosexual scene of Stevenson's day without being explicit is particularly strongly pursued by Wayne Koestenbaum and Elaine Showalter.[21] Koestenbaum is highly alert to any possible gay hints and implications in the text and is very possibly correct in believing that many of the first readers would have suspected Jekyll's transgressions and desires as being homosexual ones. Before the final revelation they will have thought this to be the likely truth about the relationship between the title characters. Koesten-baum's discussion goes far beyond *Jekyll and Hyde*, however, to the whole matter of Stevenson's collaborations, above all with Lloyd Osbourne in *The Ebb-Tide* which is given an equally detailed examination in search of verbal hints and clues. Indeed, Koestenbaum's main point is that Stevenson himself was a homosexual and that his collaborations with Osbourne and with Henley reflect the fact – as does Stevenson's periodic resentful-ness of Fanny's natural role in constricting his freedom. Showalter is also prepared to entertain the possibility that Stevenson was gay, but her main emphasis is on the tale being what she describes as 'a fable of fin-de-siècle homosexual panic', the near-hysteria which (she says) gripped the world of male clubland at that time.

Another frequently encountered line of discussion is to see the tale, like so many other works of the period, as reflecting the deep insecurities seething below the apparent stability of late Victorian Britain. Linda Dryden has been particularly exhaustive in outlining the contemporary fears it may be drawing upon.[22] She too notes the flavour of homosexuality in the story, but focuses more upon the unsettling suspicion of a general degeneracy which had invaded the thinking of the time in reaction to the earlier Victorian assumption of human progress. Stevenson's age was aware of possible degeneracy both at the level of the individual and in mob behaviour; more radically still, they contemplated the idea that the race itself might be degenerating, and that society might fall apart. One particular suspicion involved the idea that criminals are a 'type' and a throwback to a primitive stage in human evolution, a notion which gave rise to the idea of the 'morally insane'. Most alarming of all, perhaps, was the fear that moral insanity might not be confined to the lower classes but might also emerge in the upper levels of society. Respectability itself, in other words, seemed fragile: mingled with this alarm was the mistrust of the other races which were more and more in evidence particularly in London's East End, and the underlying suspicion that if British respectability was vulnerable, then the racial superiority upon which the Empire itself could be justified was vulnerable also. This maelstrom of insecurity found its natural focus in the ungraspable life of London itself, with all its vastness and variety – for this reason alone, Dryden sees London as the true location of *Jekyll and Hyde*, rather than Edinburgh as has occasionally been suggested. Stephen Arata also had explored similar possibilities regarding aristocratic degeneration in an earlier study which contains a further valuable examination of the tale.[23]

Dryden's exploration of the idea of degeneracy has been echoed by Julia Reid, though her discussion stresses more the instabilities of social conditions and the emerging pressures for further democratic change.[24] She is helpful, too, in showing the story's engagement with the 'new sciences' – she lists criminology, criminal anthropology, evolutionist psychiatry, and sexology, and reminds us that there was much awareness at the time of multiple levels of consciousness. Nor are these writers alone in approaching *Jekyll and Hyde* from angles derived from various aspects of life at that time. Sara Clayson, for example, sees in it reflections of Victorian spiritualist ideas and practices, while relating them (as so many other commentators do, whatever their particular emphases) back to the unsettling arrival of Darwinism.[25] Thomas L. Reed, Jr., however, is concerned with a different social problem: alcoholism. Viewing and selecting from the text through that particular prism – it is remarkable how this story lends itself verbally to a wide variety of readings through a number of intellectual spectacles – Reed firmly interprets Jekyll as (essentially) an alcoholic and goes on to see Stevenson himself as, at best, a near-alcoholic, thanks to the large number of alcohol references which can be found throughout his writing.[26]

Very different again is Mark Currie who considers it in narratological terms.[27] Currie's goal is essentially a theoretical one but in reaching it he subjects the story to a fresh and detailed scrutiny: his starting-point is the implications of Henry Jekyll's telling of his own story. To Currie, the text is ultimately inscrutable, which is why it is open to such a particularly wide range of readings and responses. The point is made again by Roger Luckhurst as the final words of the introduction for his recent edition – which may also serve as our final words on the subject: 'A text like *Jekyll and Hyde* is over-determined by multiple and often contradictory elements: its final meaning will always be running ahead of us, ducking round the corner like Mr Hyde, forever just out of reach.' (*JH* xxxii)

'THE MISADVENTURES OF JOHN NICHOLSON' (WRITTEN 1885–6)

Few people seem to have much of a good word for 'The Misadventures of John Nicholson', begun in 1885 but largely written in the winter of 1886. It was eventually published in *Yule Tide*, Cassell's Christmas Annual of 1887. The leading disparager was arguably Stevenson himself. 'I have been writing much verse, quite the bard, in fact; and also a dam tale to order, which will be what it will be; I don't love it, but some of it is passable in its mouldy way, "The Misadventures of John Nicholson", it hight.'[28] This comment to Colvin, on 14 December 1886, was matched by a similarly jaundiced comment to Henry James on 23 December: 'I am really a very fair sort of a fellow all things considered, have done some work; a silly Xmas story (with some larks in it) which won't be out till I don't know when.' (Mehew 326) And the tone is maintained five years later, in October or November 1891, when he was writing from Vailima to Henry

Baildon, whose Edinburgh house at Murrayfield Stevenson had imagined as the scene of the murder in the story: 'Did you see a silly tale, "John Nicholson's Predicament" – or some such name – in which I had made free with your house at Murrayfield?' (Mehew 474)

Compared with the works he was also writing at this time, *Jekyll and Hyde* and *Kidnapped*, 'John Nicholson' is indeed a light and fantastic thing – indeed, essentially a joke, with its chain of comic disasters. Poor John Nicholson seems to be totally hapless whenever he is in the environs of Edinburgh. (He seems to be far less hapless while in California.) It was indeed a piece of work 'to order', as Stevenson strove to earn his living from his pen. He was working on it, also, while under even heavier than usual family strains, especially as his father's health was declining: Thomas Stevenson would die soon after, on 8 May 1887.

More recent commentators have scarcely been more kind. Several omit it completely from their accounts of Stevenson's life and works; others see it as principally significant for the clarity with which it reflects that lifelong problem of Stevenson's which had become particularly pressing once more, namely his relationship with his father. We can scarcely avoid seeing much of Thomas Stevenson (or at least his son's perception of him) in Mr Nicholson, that strict, unbending, utterly respectable businessman and adherent of the Free Kirk, who keeps his sons on such a tight rein, especially where money is concerned. And what remains that is not to be laid specifically at Thomas Stevenson's door is doubtless merely a distillation of Stevenson's view of the rigidities of Presbyterian Edinburgh as a whole. Equally near-certain is the origin (though not the fate) of John Nicholson's scapegrace friend Alan Houston in Stevenson's cousin Bob, so disapproved of by Stevenson's father. If we read the father-son tale in relationship to Stevenson's life, then it is a vision of faults on both sides, with the father's blinkered limitations counterpointed against the son's bumbling transgressions and misfortunes. Indeed, the story may contain echoes of even more of the circumstances then plaguing Stevenson. Both Fanny and her son Lloyd seemed suspiciously liable to illnesses of dubious severity, just like John Nicholson's sister Maria at the end of the tale. And the maturing – or the decline –

of the original enchantingly youthful Flora into the ultra-capable, managing (and plain-faced) woman John eventually leads to the altar may be a response to the realities of Stevenson's own marriage. The respectable world of the Nicholsons is undoubtedly a jaundiced vision of the world in which Stevenson grew up, right down to its 'frigid dinner-parties' (XII, JN 178).

Yet it seems insufficient to scan the story merely for glimpses of its author's own life. Stevenson may have felt it to be hack-work, but it surely succeeds in entertaining on its own account. It is the work of a (by this time) consummate professional writer and stylist: Stevenson may have thought it akin to drudgery, but he nevertheless produced a very readable entertainment in this admittedly improbable narrative (but then, so is *Treasure Island*) which is told with such inventive zest and verbal liveliness. And one has the impression that, if nothing else, he finds pleasure in re-inhabiting Edinburgh and his own childhood and youth. No other substantial work of his conducts the reader through the streets of his native city so extensively or precisely as does this one, although *Catriona* runs it close. The Edinburgh of *Catriona*, however, is the Edinburgh of the visitor and of history; the Edinburgh of 'John Nicholson' is the city of Stevenson's childhood memories and student escapades, and the result is an environment in which sheer ordinariness can transform itself into extraordinary disaster in the twinkling of an eye – just as childhood lives can, from second to second. The unexpected, the flip-side of normality, presses very close here: the romance of the everyday turns in a flash into an everyday nightmare. So, poor John's doom is caused merely by his omitting to remove the money he should have banked from his coat pocket when he hung it up. Similarly, a door which locks automatically when shut, a lack of change in one's pocket to tip a railway porter, even the affability of a friendly cabbie – all can conspire, in this story, to entrap the unfortunate hero until his predicament seems almost insuperable. John Nicholson and Edinburgh are fitted to each other like hand and glove, and simultaneously are utterly at odds. Similarly, the Edinburgh of 'John Nicholson' is a place where the merest tissue separates respectable and culpable behaviour: the disaster-generating world of Alan Hudson consists of a billiard-emporium which merely transports the game from the respectable homes of the New Town to a parent-free zone. Similarly, Collette's shebeen is equally free of parents and of strict adherence to legal hours, though a favourite with sections of the legal fraternity itself. In this world of confusion about what is permitted and advisable, transgression is as easy as it is disastrous. The tale is a comic, highly exaggerated but vividly imagined nightmare of the malevolence of the normal.

That is a ponderously adult way of saying that John's adventure is essentially a child's story given an adult disguise. At the end, Flora rightly accuses John of essentially childish behaviour: 'You got into trouble, and when your father, honest man, was disappointed, you took the pet, or got afraid, and ran away from punishment.' (JN 214) John's note to his father, as he quits his home for the other side of the world, is a hilariously juvenile effusion: 'You will never hear of me again.' (JN 171) The reason why the tale is simultaneously so solidly real and so surrealistically improbable – so Stevensonian, in fact – is the way it creates an adult world through a child's sensibility. This is not a matter, however, of the author failing to grow up (as some critics of an earlier generation seemed to suspect): rather, it is an instance of an author adopting a comic fictional vision in which narrative is prioritized, and choosing one of the worlds of narrative (in this case, the world as experienced by a child) which he finds personally congenial. Stevenson had several such.

Such an extraordinary concatenation of mishaps, of sheer rotten luck, can scarcely avoid hinting at a certain malevolence in the nature of things. Not that the tale has anything of the profundity to which Hardy might aspire: jokiness easily prevails here over philosophy and the outcome is far from tragic. Yet the reader can hardly avoid thinking that someone, or something, 'has it in for' John. Stevenson will soon set out to create a serious tale in which fate, or doom, will play a part: *Weir of Hermiston*. Here, the question of where the fault for, or cause of, all these misadventures is to be found is lightly touched upon only towards the end, when John's re-discovered Flora, now a nurse in early middle age, responds to his story by ordering him down on his knees to pray to God for forgiveness. John does so, though with a caveat: 'But while he was heartily enough requesting forgiveness on general principles, the rational side of him distinguished, and wondered if, perhaps, the apology were not due upon the other part.' (*JN* 214) When he dares to suggest, however, that very little in the way of fault on his part has caused these events, he is roundly told off for some of the standard failings of a scapegrace: he had not written home, he had drunk too much, he had flounced off, pettishly fleeing from punishment. (And the vision of the child-in-the-wrong is completed by the fantasy of returning to the family bosom having done something wonderful which will 'show them'. Only, as usually happens in real life, the triumphant return is instantly deflated by the renewed encounter with family reality.) Flora's vision is of the soundness of bourgeois morality as a fence against a world of ill-fortune: Stevenson is humorously acknowledging the local advantages of his parents' values. Yet the reader's sympathy remains with John, just as (in the same way) we cheer the spirit of rebellion and adventure in his creator. Fortunately, it is a comedy, after all, and the faults ascribed to him are merely those which bourgeois parents have always deplored in their growing offspring. The something which has it in for John is merely the unpredictable but malign world which anxious parents of 'well-brought-up' children try to save them from, a world which the parental vision goes a long way to actually create.

Stevenson's evidence for the capacity of a scapegrace to survive misadventures rests, most firmly of all, on the sheer ironic verve of his own writing. There is a cheerful impudence in the biblical references of the chapter titles, and in the gentle but pervasive inflations of language gesturing towards the poetic, the epic, and the tragic. Above all, Stevenson's ability simply to find language to evoke inner sensation, or to tease out a situation, is working at its best. As always, Stevenson's writing provides its own pleasure, and contributes to a satiric vision which gently criticizes Edinburgh's ethos of Christian respectability while half-acknowledging the culpability of those (in effect, most of sinning mankind) who step outside it. It is a winning formula for entertaining, satiric narrative which, whether it means to or not, looks back at Byron and forward to Eric Linklater.

KIDNAPPED (WRITTEN 1886)

Kidnapped offers such pure narrative pleasure that it can seem unnecessary to analyse or criticize it. Along with *Treasure Island*, it is likely to strike the reader as the quintessence of Stevenson's ability in captivating tale-telling. Within its first half-dozen lines, a sense of story-beginning and narrative direction has set in. The adventure is told so confidently – its first-person narration poised between a lucidity which has presented little difficulty to generations of young readers and just enough idiosyncrasy to suggest the thinking and reminiscing of a late-eighteenth-century Scottish adult – that the tale exists magnificently as both a 'children's classic' and a substantial historical novel worthy of at least being mentioned in the same breath as those of Scott. Certainly, that twin perception, that it is for both young boys and adults alike, is visible in the book's first reviews and responses. It cannot simply be ghettoized as a book for children. On the other hand, one should not play down or ignore its appeal to the young. Its narrative excitement, its romance emphasis on adventure, and its escape into history and wild landscape mean that its kinship with *Treasure Island* is unavoidable. The heart of the tale, the 'flight in the heather', is a narrative of extreme outdoor survival, classic entertainment for children: it is a kind of deadly Duke of Edinburgh's Award challenge. David and Alan are scouting, admittedly, not for boys, but for the many enemies who surround them: their reward is not a badge but an escape from the gallows. This threat, however, only raises the imaginative excitement. Furthermore, it is a young person's book in that it is short compared with most Victorian novels for adults, falling into brief and clear-cut episodes, most of which have a powerful imaginative life of their own. *Kidnapped* was never going to be part of Leavis's Great Tradition. On the other hand, it is a poor soul who, however sophisticated, cannot take pleasure in this book. The solidity of its rendering of a historical Scottish place and time means that it essentially repeats Walter Scott's winning formula: the knowledgeable accuracy with which the world of David and Alan greets the reader is applied to a distanced, escapist world of the eighteenth-century Scottish Highlands, so that romance and realism are simultaneously, and compellingly, on offer.

Nor, perhaps, is its appeal to be seen as confined to men and boys. It also seems to work for women and girls, despite the absence of important female characters. Muriel Spark seemed to think so: her Sandy Stranger, the eventual betrayer of Jean Brodie, has schoolgirl daydreams of fleeing loyally through the heather with Alan Breck. (One of David's temptations is to abandon Alan in the interests of his own safety, but he rejects this as a betrayal of the loyalty he feels he owes to the charismatic and complex figure who has so decisively entered his life; Sandy, on the other hand, eventually feels no compunction in rejecting and betraying the charismatic and complex figure who has played such a major part in hers. Loyalty is a theme in both Edinburgh-derived works.) And if the fictional Sandy Stranger seems doubtful evidence for the book's appeal to girls, we might remind ourselves that among the most recent and persuasive advocates of the book have been Jenni Calder and Emma Letley.

In part, the story's narrative power is achieved by its conformity to some of the most basic and reliable of narrative types and devices: the youth setting out on the adventure of life, the heir striving to claim his inheritance, the long journey across a landscape full of the wondrous, the dangerous, and the unexpected. This fact, obvious to any experienced reader, is regularly but tellingly underlined by the text itself, first of all in Chapter 4: David begins to suspect his miserly uncle of being like the ballad-character of the 'wicked kinsman that tried to keep him from his own'.[29] A little later, the seaman Riach declares that David's kidnapping by his uncle 'was like a ballad' (K. 45); while on the run, David's image of the gallows which threaten him is derived from 'the top of a pedlar's ballad' (K. 111); and as the fleeing pair contrive to cross the Forth so that David can gain access to the lawyer Rankeillor, he once again sees himself striving 'to claim my inheritance, like a hero in a ballad' (K. 166). Finally, David's eventual triumph is confirmed with 'So the beggar in the ballad had come home' (K. 191). Rankeillor, too, is struck by the narrative power and typicality of David's story, but his parallels are with a more exalted version of balladry: he sees the tale as a 'great epic, a great Odyssey' (K. 178). These comparisons, of course, are retailed by the older, mature David as he tells his own story, but he talks of them as

85

having occurred in the mind of his young self as the adventure was being lived through: the ballad comparisons help characterize the young man who has just recently left childhood, just as the Homeric comparison helps characterize the lawyer. (Rankeillor is one of Scottish fiction's learned pedants, but Stevenson is far more deft than the creator of Baron Bradwardine, knowing how to avoid taxing his reader's patience with an excess of comic eccentricity.) But the comparisons with balladry are not just in the minds of characters: the novel really is shaped, powerfully, by ballad patterns and elements.

As just hinted, *Kidnapped* has an obvious precursor and, to some extent, a model in Scott's *Waverley* (1814). In each, an inexperienced young man makes a journey through the Scottish Highlands, finding that the region's ways, culture, history, and tensions are not like anything he has imagined before, and challenging and threatening to his very life. His principal guide and mentor in the region is a charismatic and potentially dangerous friend, prominent among the Highlanders. Each, after various wild adventures, returns to a place in Lowland society, many of the difficulties in the way having been cleared by a wise and capable senior friend who embodies crucial Lowland virtues. That said, the comparison with *Waverley* is most instructive in highlighting what *Kidnapped* is apparently *not* about. Unlike Scott's novel, *Kidnapped* is not overtly concerned with the shape and meaning of the larger history of eighteenth-century Scotland: it is not a historical novel in the deep sense of a novel which overtly sets out to inform us about history, and interpret it for us. Stevenson is clearly sufficiently knowledgeable about the history of the period and the region, but the book makes little attempt to relate that history to Scotland's larger tale, whereas Scott's book (like so many other Waverley novels) is all about the unfolding history of Scotland, at one level at least. Stevenson makes great use of his detailed historical and cultural knowledge, but he has no grand interpretation of it to offer, as Scott had.

That said, it is clearly possible to see it as reflecting the different historical circumstances of Scott and Stevenson, at either end of the nineteenth century. For Scott, it was appropriate to write fiction which confronted Scotland's place in history in his lifetime. A century after the Union of the

Parliaments, and with Scots ever more conscious of how the lives of the two nations were growing closer together under the political umbrella, Scott (like so many others of his generation) could appreciate how Scottish distinctiveness was eroding within the British identity and could still feel how there was further scope for the Union to become confirmed in hearts on both sides of the border. His fictions contrive to celebrate and maintain as much of Scottish history and individuality as possible, while confirming the appropriateness, the rightness, of the Union. Equally, his writings helped create a knowledge, and love of Scotland amongst his southern compatriots. He was writing about a still living tension, in other words, within Scotland, within Britain, and within himself. By the time Stevenson was writing in the 1880s, the tension seems to have relaxed: for late-Victorian Scots in general, Britishness was no longer an issue. The case no longer had to be made. What had made the difference? One is tempted to say, Time and Balmoral – and also Scott. And so Stevenson could write his novel about a Whig and a Jacobite co-operating to survive, and confronting their common enemies – the hardships of the natural world, the perils of chance and fate, the cruelty and injustice of men – rather than each other. The novel is concerned, as usual with Stevenson, with the experience of life, not with the direction of history.

Equally, it would not appear to be a novel about the education and growth to adulthood of its hero, despite our natural expectations. At the outset, David is certainly youthful and inexperienced, but his adventure lasts around two and a half months merely, and at the end, although he has had a plethora of experiences in that time, he is, and seems, just as youthful as ever. He has certainly had no major revolution in his attitudes to compare with Waverley's breakthrough to maturity on the shores of Ullswater. Nor is there any great emphasis, at the outset, on youthful faults and limitations which life will have to knock out of him, whereas Waverley's highly cloistered upbringing and his immature emotional and imaginative experiences are patiently laid before us in those notorious early chapters of Scott's first novel. Perhaps the worst one can say about the David of the early pages of *Kidnapped* is that he is too ready to assume that he has mastered a situation (as when he first checkmates his uncle), insufficiently aware of what the world, and human behaviour in particular, might yet throw at him. The book's concern, however, is always precisely with what the world throws at him: David's challenge is to survive by responding to the surprises of each new episode, and to make his way, against all the circumstances ranged against him by malice and chance, to the goal which (as in a folk-tale) it is natural and appropriate that he should achieve, namely the inheritance of the estate of Shaws. That this should be the essential pattern is thoroughly appropriate for a book designed for the young – for those, in other words, who stand at the threshold of adult life and who wonder (consciously or unconsciously) what the world has in store for them, and how they will cope. Stevenson's tale projects that universal situation, and provides a reassuring fictional account of inexperience eventually surmounting life's challenges, partly as a result of youth's deep-seated energy, optimism, and instinct to thrive, and partly through sheer good fortune.

The centrality of the flight in the heather crystallizes how this is a tale in which youthful vulnerability is pitted against the violent reality of a world which the young, in their innocence, can scarcely imagine. It is not solely David who carries this theme as he first sets off from Essendean. The striking figure of Ransome, the child sailor, is both comically and tragically a member of the kidnapping crew, his tender age corrupted by the life he has to lead. He appears in the story just as David thinks that in checkmating his uncle he has triumphed over life's hazards. Ransome, so soon to die himself, symbolizes David's innocence as he journeys to the fateful destination of the Hawes Inn. Ransome's death is shocking, but it is only a portion of the violence and horror with which Stevenson endows his world of eighteenth-century Scotland. The realistic violence of the defence of the ship's round-house, the fate of the drowning sailors trapped in the sinking brig, the vivid brevity of the account of the Red Fox's dying moments, the detailed conviction of the hardships David experiences as he journeys with Alan – all convey the truth of the violent and dangerous adult world the young hero has to survive in. Less physical and immediate are Stevenson's other reminders of the harshness of Highland life at that time: the hardship and injustice to which the people are often exposed, and the deep sadness of the encounter with the emigrant ship at the beginning of Chapter 16. In those few months, David Balfour may not change a lot, but he certainly sees and learns a lot.

The view of David as someone who does not grow up over the course of the novel has been elaborately explored by Alan Sandison, who reads *Kidnapped* as 'a novel of arrested development'.[30] Sandison detects psychological weakness, either in David or his author, or both, and although his discussion is full of detailed and sensitive readings, it is likely that many of *his* readers will be unwilling to share his deep discontent with David's failure, within the confines of the novel, to achieve a fully independent adult spiritual status. In Sandison's view, David has a problem; to others of us, David's innocence of the world may appear to be entirely explicable (he has been brought up in rural seclusion, raised by a father, and watched over by a fatherly clergyman, who seem to have been equally innocent and unworldly), and furthermore we may also feel that he does not make such a bad fist of surviving in these first few months of journeying into a peculiarly dangerous world for which none of his childhood father-figures had prepared him. Indeed, if David does not seem fully adult, we might find part of the explanation in what we are told of the generation before him: neither his father nor his youthful uncle, in Rankeillor's account, were totally finished, sensible men fully equal to the demands of adult maturity and confident social living. Their behaviour, in their very different ways, was childish with consequences detrimental to themselves, their family, and their dependants; David, for all his immaturity, bids fair to grow up better than either of them.

And his immaturity creates situations that even the book's younger readers can appreciate. This is particularly true of the chief instance of moral and psychological tension, the quarrel between the two principal characters: while Alan is certainly in the wrong, and limited in his appreciation of the nature, extent and effect of his wrongdoing, it is David's youthful pride which creates the essential problem between them and which delays its resolution. Like a young child, David nurses his sense of grievance, finding it impossible to break out of the moody stance in which he becomes trapped. He even slips into the childishness of looking forward to his own death as a punishment for his opponent, thinking: 'When I lie down and die, you will feel it like a buffet in your face; ah, what a revenge!' (*K*. 154) Alan is right when he castigates himself for forgetting that David is 'just a bairn', though it has to be said that he has behaved (not for the first time) rather childishly himself. These characters possess inner psychological diversity but far from excessive complexity, and their moral dilemmas are clear-cut and largely momentary, requiring little or nothing in the way of slow, narrative unfolding.

Against Sandison's dissatisfaction with David, a dissatisfaction that is not so concerned with Stevenson's invention of the character but, seemingly, more with the character in itself – his opening comment sets the tone: 'David Balfour tells lies about his age'[31] – we might counterpoint the preference of one of the earliest modern critics of the novel, David Daiches, for whom David is created with 'careful and unpretentious sobriety' and who regrets 'a certain thinness in the handling of Alan's character, and a shallow theatrical quality in Alan that does not represent his character so much as his creator's inability to see very deeply into it'.[32] Sandison, on the other hand, warms to Alan's vigour and endless ability to take the initiative, as opposed to the supine tendencies he detects in the young man. Neither critic, one might argue, allows for the need of younger readers to project their own feelings on to these two central figures: had either David or Alan been too completely realized, been made to 'come alive' with the fullness that Daiches hoped for, then one suspects that it would no longer have been such an effective adventure romance with a particular appeal to the young. One could claim, in any case, that Alan, with his sometimes astonishing Highland way of looking at things and his moral faults both major and minor, is complex enough to sustain our interest along with our affection. Equally, David, sufficiently the Lowland Whig to satisfy the historically expert Daiches, has the capacity – the individuality and the backbone – to take occasional and impulsive decisions which reflect both a strong, principled morality and a capacity for heroism, above all when he instinctively sides with the stranger against the crew of the *Covenant* and also when he sticks with Alan when reason suggests that it would be safer to separate from him.

Occasionally, too, other manly characters, such as the not wholly sympathetic Cluny, admit that David has spirit.

Few readers, one suspects, find themselves preferring one of the pair over the other: much of the novel's appeal rests on the way in which they become a unity, despite their apparent incompatibility. Here we find another standard narrative device, one which seems to appeal to the modern mind in particular. The adventures of a mismatched pair, thrown together by peculiar circumstances and forced to co-operate in order to survive or succeed, is now a staple of the cinema, providing the basic idea of many a western or crime movie. It is hard to think of an earlier nineteenth-century example of the pattern, however, than *Kidnapped* – except for *Huckleberry Finn*, which was published in Britain in 1884. (Eighteenth-century novels are another matter.) *Kidnapped* was being written very soon afterwards, and it is tempting to think that Twain's book, a great favourite of Stevenson's, played a part in its genesis. If this novel features, prominently, a mismatched pair, one might argue that a great deal of Stevenson's writing has to do with mismatched pairs. However, Stevenson's instinctive concern with doubles, and with the divided self, is particularly pervasive in this work. It takes the form of splits of various kinds, internal contradictions, within most of the characters including the crew of the *Covenant* (even kidnapper-in-chief Hoseason has a benign shore personality and a ruthless sea-going one: villain as he is, he remains a loving son to his aged mother). And the heart of many of these divisions is to be found in the overarching division with which the novel deals, Highland and Lowland.

Stevenson may not share Scott's concern with the direction of history, but he is certainly Scott's heir in his interest in the diversity of cultures which Scotland has always contained, never more strikingly than in the eighteenth century. Daiches is clearly correct in implying that Stevenson, brought up in mid-nineteenth-century Edinburgh, had a natural knowledge of the mental and cultural world of Enlightenment Scotland, and he may also be correct in believing that Stevenson's sense of the Highlands was more superficial, a matter of stock assumptions and prejudices. That said, we must credit Stevenson with an interest in post-Culloden Highland culture which goes beyond the needs of a juvenile adventure story, and it is this which, in large part, justifies regarding it as a historical novel in the shadow of Scott. If Stevenson cannot fully satisfy the historian, he has nevertheless created a 'Highland' world which fully serves the purposes of a novel. David's journeys bring him into contact with a wide range of Highland characters and types, as well as several historical figures. Stevenson's knowledge of the history of the Highlands was considerable (he intended, for a time, to write a history of the region). Furthermore, the sense of sympathy for the ordinary Highlanders, oppressed and fearful in the immediate aftermath of Culloden, is strong, nowhere more so than in the encounter with the emigrant ship. Alan, after the roundhouse fight, begins the process of initiating David into the harsh realities of contemporary Highland life, an understanding which David is soon able to improve, partly through further discussion with the sympathetic catechist Henderland and partly through his own experiences with the predominantly kindly Highland folk. As Julia Reid has argued, the novel contradicts what was no doubt still the predominant nineteenth-century prejudice regarding the Highlands, namely that, left to its own devices, it was a region which would remain stuck in physical, economic, and cultural primitivism but which was steadily benefiting from the onward march of time and Lowland civilization.[33] Stevenson's picture oozes sympathy for a people who are in cultural confusion, economic hardship, and threatened with violence. It is remarkable how little of the Romantic and Victorian glorification of the Highlands is to be found in these pages.

Behind David and Alan, the central duality, lie the differences between the two Scottish worlds which produced them. Nevertheless, the cultural contrast between the two characters cannot be separated from the more narrowly psychological differences between them. Indeed, to a large extent these are one and the same. If one discounts the cultural element in their make-up, by and large one is left merely with the differences in their ages and experience of life. The motif of the mismatched pair, wherever it crops up, usually draws most of its strength and entertainment value from just such a radical clash of cultures. It is a formula rich in possibilities of humour, adventure, and striking situations. It is also a paradoxical idea: at one level it emphasizes cultural diversity and division within society, or within a nation. At another level, it implies unity: the combined efforts of the diverse pair striving for a common goal can suggest that the society (or nation) is not so broken after all, and that a shared humanity underlies the spiky differences which produce so much of the tension, and fun.

That sense of *Kidnapped*, with its sequel *Catriona*, expressing fundamental perceptions about the lives both of the individual and of the nation, lies near the root of the response of the scholar and critic who has worked on these books, in recent years, most fruitfully of all, Barry Menikoff.[34] In both his edition of *Kidnapped* and his more recent monograph, Menikoff has made the case which has occasionally tempted other writers to see *Kidnapped* as Stevenson's most successful, perhaps his 'greatest', novel. His praise of *Kidnapped* in particular rests on his vivid sense of its inherent artistry, and his view of the two novels together is far more unified than that of most readers (who sometimes view *Catriona* as a slightly unexpected extension of *Kidnapped* which resulted in a more problematical novel). For Menikoff, the two together form a national epic enriched by far more historical and legal scholarship (on Stevenson's part) than readers realize. His view is radical: 'Both in the impulse that intuited a major subject in an old crime, and in the technique that brought that idea to life, Stevenson paved the way for later writers like Truman Capote, Norman Mailer, and W. G. Sebald.'[35]

Others may be content to say that if *Kidnapped* has a meaning which elevates it above the status of 'mere' entertainment for children, it must be a meaning which speaks both to the young and adult readers who have cherished it over the years. It is a meaning which reflects the book's peculiar ability to seem both juvenile and adult at the same time, for I do not believe that different age groups read it in radically different ways. Children reading it do not struggle to read an 'adult' fiction; adults reading it are not regressing, guiltily, to childhood as they turn to it once more. Its peculiar centrality and universality of appeal is related to the ambiguity of David's status in the spectrum of human life: he is both a child and a man. For Sandison, as we have seen, this means that he is someone who fails, strangely, to develop. For other readers, however, this ambiguity is what makes him universally appealing and relevant. His story, of encountering life's surprises (to put it mildly) and of confronting and overcoming them, thereby making progress to the goal of safety and security in one's chosen society, is relevant both to young and old. The young reader who may yet have to deal with life outwith the shelter of a home made by others is here confronted, imaginatively, with the task of mastering it; the older reader should appreciate characters encountering life's challenges and their constant effort to retain the stable happiness and security we all seek. It is easy to mock David (or Stevenson) for heading his second chapter 'I Come to my Journey's End', as if the book's conclusion had been reached, for of course it is ironic at that point – but will eventually be true, as the climax of the book, the thwarting of Ebenezer on that same spot, shows. The goal is always at hand, only life has a way of interposing itself between us and it, and of snatching us away again. The image of kidnapping articulates how, in life, experience can thwart a natural, comfortable progression and consists, rather, of a succession of problems, large or small, to be overcome. There is a perpetual tension between our desires and our actuality. Life constantly kidnaps us.

4

'Voices in the Darkness'

The phrase was Henry James's, in a letter to Stevenson of 21 October 1893 (Maixner 440–1). Full of praise for *Catriona*, he nevertheless regretted what he felt as the absence of visual description in the novel. 'The one thing I miss in the book is the note of *visibility* – it subjects my visual sense, my *seeing* imagination, to an almost painful underfeeding', he says, and he finds himself, as he reads, 'in the presence of voices in the darkness.' Stevenson responded to this in a letter of early December of that same year (Mehew 565–6), agreeing with James's perception but scarcely apologetic:

> 'Tis true, and unless I make the greater effort – and am, as a step to that, convinced of its necessity – it will be more true I fear in the future. I *hear* people talking, and I *feel* them acting, and that seems to me to be fiction. My two aims may be described as –
> 1st. War to the adjective.
> 2nd. Death to the optic nerve.

When he wrote this he had already completed and sent off what was to be his last finished work, *The Ebb-Tide*. What remained were unfinished fragments, because a year later, almost to the day, he would suddenly die. His letter looks to a future which might have been. In it, he is asserting what he knows are his strengths, in the invented actions of his characters, and in how they, and his narrators, 'speak'. When necessary, he can provide rich enough scenic descriptions, as his two great tales from the South Seas show. His last works have each an especially strong sense of place, in fact, but it derives primarily from the characters themselves, from their words and deeds, and from the stories told about them, rather than from extensive descriptions.

The sense that his writings written after he left Britain for the Americas in 1887, so memorable and full of creative energy, are 'late' or 'last' works should be resisted, and one's consciousness that darkness would soon engulf their author's voice should be kept at bay. It is only in retrospect that death appears to engulf the voices in his stories; though they were among the last things he was to write, there is nothing elegiac about them, nothing of the supposed serenity or calm maturity of old age. They just stop, in mid-sentence.

In a way, it was death which gave him the spur to whole new vistas of life. His father died in May 1887 and three months later the Stevenson family, which now included his widowed mother, crossed the Atlantic. This first phase of westward travel took them to the Adirondacks in upper New York State, a place of hard winters. The following year, the continent was crossed and they took ship to the South Seas, on a cruise of exploration with a view to writing a new travel book. They reached Samoa late in 1889, where they purchased the estate which would be Stevenson's final home. To his circle of literary friends, it seemed astonishing that he should banish himself so completely, though Samoa provided at least workable communications with Europe and the rest of the world. Stevenson remained in active contact with friends and business contacts in Britain and America, but this 'isolation' showed as never before the independence of his imagination and of his work habits. And if Samoa prompted some very vivid recreations of the Scotland he had lost and would probably never see again, it also stimulated him to a fresh concern with the political, economic, and cultural spheres of human activity, as he observed the detailed workings of colonialism.

THE MASTER OF BALLANTRAE (WRITTEN 1887–9)

Recent years have seen a shift in our understanding and assessment of *The Master of Ballantrae*. Where once the focus was almost solely on the two brothers and the implications and interpretative possibilities of their different temperaments and mutual antagonism, an alternative duality has crept into the discussion and with it a different focus of interpretation.

Ephraim Mackellar has long been recognized as a fascinating and convincing character in his own right, and the effectiveness of his employment as the narrator of much of the story has always been accepted. Nevertheless, earlier critics were unlikely to have located him at the core of the novel: he has traditionally been seen as an inspired aspect of narrative method, the product of Stevenson's ability to create a character through its style of speech, rather than as lying at the centre of the book's meaning. Critics such as Alan Sandison and Adrian Poole, however, now focus on Mackellar as crucial to the novel Stevenson produced.[1] For them, the principal dualism is the opposition of James Durie and Mackellar, not that of Henry and James: in these readings, the book's great tussle is a contest between James and Mackellar for Henry's life and soul. And the fact that such drastically different emphases are possible is a reflection of the book's diverse and conflicted nature.

For an earlier critic, David Daiches, *The Master of Ballantrae* was a late, but still flawed, step on the path to the mature achievement of the regrettably unfinished *Weir of Hermiston*.[2] It is a work caught, we were told, between a memorable rendering of the psychological human drama played out in the Scottish scenes, and the regrettable adventure story episodes with their glimpses of the Master's worldwide wanderings. The book's notorious conclusion abandons Scotland entirely, climaxing in a preposterous mechanical resolution of the brothers' mutual destructiveness: the failing Henry dies of shock as he beholds a last flicker of life in the brother he has just watched being dug up from the grave. Earlier critics such as Daiches saw Stevensonian dualism not merely in certain pairs of characters, or in interior psychological conflicts, but also in his oscillation between episodes of boyish escapism as opposed to the maturity of more 'adult' portions elsewhere.

More recent critics seem to be less concerned with funda-mental flaws: two have focused on questions of literary influence. Eric Massie explored the relationship between *The Master of Ballantrae* and the work which haunts quite a lot of our thinking about Stevenson's inspiration generally, James Hogg's *The Private Memoirs and Confessions of a Justified Sinner* (1824).[3] Massie provides a detailed and sensible discussion of the similarities between Hogg's novel and Stevenson's, though he does not regard it as Stevenson's only source. Somewhat more unexpected, however, is Hilary J. Beattie's article in which she digs deeply into the friendship between Stevenson and Henry James.[4] This account ranges much further than the usual discussion of the essays in which the famous pair argue about the nature of fiction, and considers what influences from each might be discerned in the fictions of the other, as well as possible reflections of their real-life circumstances. Beattie finds a surprising amount of James in *The Master of Ballantrae*, starting with the names of the brothers and possibly also including echoes of *Portrait of a Lady* (despite Stevenson's lack of enthusiasm for that particular James novel). She also suspects that memories of Stevenson continued to haunt James long after the Scotsman's death.

Stevenson himself confided to James that he was conscious of his new novel being a mix of impressive tragedy, well achieved, and portions which were

> not so soundly designed: I almost hesitate to write them; they are very picturesque, but they are fantastic, they shame, perhaps degrade, the beginning. I wish I knew; that was how the tale came to me however. ...For the third supposed death [of James Durie, when he is dug from the frozen grave] and the manner of the third reappearance is steep; steep, sir. It is even very steep, and I fear it shames the honest stuff so far. (late January 1888; Mehew 357–8)

If this was the author's view, then it is perhaps permissible to regard the tale of the two brothers as compelling, until Stevenson fumbles it towards the end. It has become possible, however, to view the interest of the novel as lying, to a considerable extent, in the drama of Mackellar's subjective recounting of the family story, and of his perception of his own role in it. As a character, he is created with considerable thoroughness, in his solid Lowland Whiggishness, his Enlightenment rationalism, his Calvinism. As such, he is clearly as much of an opposite to James as Henry is – if anything, he is even more markedly wedded to duty (as opposed to James's selfish irresponsibility) than his master and ally is. As the family tragedy deepens, with the duel and the flight to America, Mackellar becomes ever more proactive until the climactic moment of his murder attempt at sea. In the end, he is the last active member of the family he has so identified with and of which he has become a member, creating the monument to the two brothers with the words which close the novel, and writing the history which constitutes the work we read. (As the fictional preface – not reproduced in all editions of the novel – makes clear, the children of Henry and Alison simply fade to nothing.) With this perspective, even the opening words in which Mackellar justifies his recounting of the family tragedy become suspect: has 'the world' really been agog for the full truth of this odd matter, or is Mackellar shaping and declaring a history which explains, justifies, and confirms his now dominant position as the surviving embodiment of the family's life? And once the reader has shaken off much of one's initial naïve trust in Mackellar and his judgements, then the tale he is telling becomes ever more fascinating, as tales usually do which utilize untrustworthy narrators. Can we be sure, even, that James is (to put it crudely) as wicked as all that?

Stevenson's intentions as regards James Durie are fairly clear, admittedly: his letter to Colvin (24 December 1887; Mehew 356) says that 'the Master is all I know of the devil' and goes on to talk of James's 'deadly, causeless duplicity'. Elsewhere, in one of the versions of the unpublished essay he wrote about *The Master of Ballantrae*, he outlines why he thought that the character who was to be revived from the grave, in the style of an Indian fakir, should be evil rather than good, while elsewhere in these fragments he indicates that the story of the family feud between the brothers, and the circumstance whereby the younger brother succeeds 'to his elder's place and future', had come to him several years previously 'on the moors between Pitlochry and Strathardle'.[5] All of which would seem to confirm the traditional reading of the work as focused on the two brothers, one of whom is 'a good man' and the other 'a kind of evil genius to his friends and family'. By Stevenson's account, the additions of Burke and Mackellar were due merely to the demands of the telling of the tale, a tale essentially centred on the four family members of the Durie household.

D. H. Lawrence's famous injunction may be relevant, however: 'Never trust the artist. Trust the tale. The proper function of a critic is to save the tale from the artist who created it.'[6] Certainly, Sandison's view that the careful reader is liable to be much in doubt while reading the novel will resonate with many, despite the apparent clarity of the story. As he points out, even the title can seem doubtful: to which character does it refer, James or Henry? Like the characters themselves, we are torn between the practical, common-sense view – that the title is Henry's, by dint of the initial agreement which was forced upon him, and the worthiness he displays in the role – and the romantic and tradition-based view – that it is James's by virtue of primogeniture and his boldly heroic and commanding personality.

Nevertheless, Stevenson's conception of two starkly different brothers trapped in a tragic enmity has a clear potential for symbolic interpretation which readers have long responded to. To some, the opposition expresses the doubleness so often ascribed (by twentieth-century commentators, at any rate) to the Scottish personality – the Caledonian antisyzygy. Equally often, it is aligned with the duality of Jekyll and Hyde, and is seen as an exploration of the splits and contradictions, the public facades and private realities, in human beings as a whole. Then again, the appropriate model might be *Kidnapped*: the divisions between Highland and Lowland Scotland, with their respective cultures and perceived temperaments, can then be invoked. If all that is not enough, the afore-mentioned contrast of the adult and the juvenile might be relevant. And there is always that most fundamental of options, of seeing the conflict as a tussle between Good and Evil, so that the tale becomes an essentially pessimistic account, as arguably *Jekyll and Hyde* is also, of how goodness is liable to be overcome by its opposite. It is one of the pleasures of the work that its interpretative potential is as varied as it is inconclusive.

It is worth stressing the pleasure which the book gives: we should qualify Daiches's sense of it as merely a large stepping-stone to a never-quite-realized maturity with the acknowledgement that it is the work of (by this time) an extremely experienced, as well as extremely gifted, writer. As he strove to bring it to a satisfying conclusion, Stevenson admitted that the task of combining two very different inspirations (the peculiar predicament of the family in the aftermath of the '45, and the weird ending in the depths of winter in upstate New York) caused him much stress and difficulty. Yet for the reader, the tale flows from beginning to end. As Adrian Poole points out,

André Gide (for one) recognized both the strange heterogeneity of the fictional material and the page-turning pleasure which it seldom fails to provide.[7] A considerable part of this is due to Mackellar or, more precisely, to his 'voice' which provides such a seemingly natural, indeed seductive, way into the tale. Stevenson's difficulties with the later stages of the action were partly bound up with the need to have this unlikely narrator recount the final lurid adventure in circumstances so far removed from his natural Scottish scene: 'this cursed end of *The Master*...is a difficult thing to write, above all in Mackellarese; and I cannot yet see my way clear', as he explained in April 1889 to the editor of *Scribner's Magazine*.[8] Yet few readers have been worried by the resulting final pages on that account at least, and so much of the book as a whole is written in a wholly satisfying manner. Time and again, Mackellar's summary distils an unfolding situation, his third-person 'recollections' felicitously punctuated (and vindicated) by deftly placed snatches of dialogue, such as this from the account of the early days of James's return to Durrisdeer:

> It was on [Henry] the burthen fell. How was he to respond to the public advances of one who never lost a chance of gibing him in private? How was he to smile back on the deceiver and the insulter? He was condemned to seem ungracious. He was condemned to silence. Had he been less proud, had he spoken, who would have credited the truth? The acted calumny had done its work; my lord and Mrs Henry were the daily witnesses of what went on; they could have sworn in court that the Master was a model of long-suffering good-nature, and Mr Henry a pattern of jealousy and thanklessness. And ugly enough as these must have appeared in any one, they seemed tenfold uglier in Mr Henry; for who could forget that the Master lay in peril of his life, and that he had already lost his mistress, his title, and his fortune?
>
> 'Henry, will you ride with me?' asks the Master one day.
>
> And Mr Henry, who had been goaded by the man all morning, raps out: 'I will not.'
>
> 'I sometimes wish you would be kinder, Henry,' says the other wistfully. (Poole 78)

Adding to the reader's pleasure is the fact that despite the story's oscillation between Scotland and far-flung places, and

101

between domestic drama and adventure narratives in distant lands, the book is a very linear one. Stevenson had produced a collage of narrative fragments in *Jekyll and Hyde* but had nevertheless created, simultaneously, a powerful narrative flow. The same skill is evident here.

The mix of geographical locations is a deeply embedded feature of the story's inspiration, and the related theme of the conflict between responsibility at home and self-satisfying, escapist wanderings abroad emerges as central. Here, clearly, is one further way of describing the contrast between the brothers. James's 'evil' at times seems to amount to no more than an extraordinary selfishness and lack of capacity to respond to the feelings of others – feelings which he nevertheless fully comprehends, hence his psychological grip on the family. Henry, on the other hand, regularly gives way to others and to the perceived human requirements of a situation. In the pair, the balance between the demands of our individuality and those of our social nature, a balance which we all live with every day, is split asunder. Distributing the opposed impulses between two characters is the step which gives the book its symbolic potential, in much the same way as the fantasy splitting of Hyde from Jekyll had done earlier. But just as the earlier tale had partially retained its link with the world of realist fiction by making Jekyll, that complex character, a familiar compound of our contradictory desires and behaviours, so Henry is allowed to possess contradictory selfish desires, stifled though they are by his sense of duty. He and Mackellar, gazing from the confines of Durrisdeer, spot the local 'free-traders' (smugglers) on the beach. ' "You would not guess what I was thinking," says he. "I was thinking I would be a happier man if I could ride and run the danger of my life with these lawless companions." ' (Poole 21) In part, the unexpected conclusion of the story, with Henry's obsessive pursuit of his brother into distant and inhospitable territory – into a wild region which is more associated with his brother's style of life – is prefigured and to some degree justified by this glimpse of Henry's inner complexity.

The opposition of Selfishness and Dutifulness may appear a rather tame domestic duo, especially as the final wild pursuit into the northern wilderness – with its echoes, perhaps, of both

Frankenstein and *Dracula* – as well as the air of mystery surrounding James's implacability (resembling, in its turn, Iago's 'motiveless malignity') prompt us to expect some rather more titanic and fundamental duality. The book, however, encompasses each realm, the mundane and the stupendous. Thus a duality of dimensions, encompassing the immediately human and the grandly universal, matches the geographical alternation between home and away, between domestic Scotland and the world of exotic danger and adventure. The book is both intimate and grandiose: its dualism goes far beyond the stark pairing of two rather different brothers.

The modern stress on Mackellar as an unreliable narrator brings home how thoroughly the novel is concerned with the relativity of perception, especially in our responses to other people. Stevenson may have made James 'all I know of the devil' but it now seems somewhat simplistic to follow the author in interpreting and judging James as purely evil and to be deplored. The reader is likely to be swayed in his favour, not so much by the sentimental elevation of his memory by the likes of the servant John Paul or Jessie Broun (whom James had originally debauched), but by the courage, insight, and resource he shows on the pirate ship and at other points in his wanderings, and also by the fact that (unlike most other characters in this deeply bleak tale) he has a sense of humour, as the curious little episode in India reveals. It may be that the attempt to come to a final, simple moral interpretation of James is doomed to failure.

In modern readings of the tale, furthermore, it is striking how Henry can become side-lined. Yet for most common readers, the story of Henry's destruction by his malign brother is likely to remain central. Stevenson's handling of Henry's slow cracking under the psychological pressure of his brother's behaviour is one of the key strengths of the book. And this theme in turn draws on another dimension not often remarked upon: the novel is Stevenson's most extensive attempt yet to depict, maturely, a married, sexually-informed relationship. (The stylized choreography of *Prince Otto* scarcely counts.) It is an unhappy – indeed, tragic – marriage, of course: just as Alison, at last, begins to fully love and support the man she has married, he begins to withdraw from the relationship as he becomes more and more obsessed with his brother. Yet Stevenson is able to make the sexual rivalry between the brothers central to the drama once James returns to Durrisdeer, and the fact that he does so is a further indication of how far he has moved from the boyishness of *Treasure Island,* or even of *Kidnapped.* Indeed, it is as if part of the impulse under which he was writing was a conscious distancing of himself from his own previous successes: these pirates are noticeably more realistic and unappealing in their brutality (with dark hints, even, of the fate of their occasional female captives) than Silver's men, while Alan Breck, who puts in what one might see as a surprise guest appearance early in the section 'The Master's Wanderings', is made to cut a less than impressive figure than at any point in *Kidnapped,* being totally outsmarted by James. Much of the novel may appear to partake of the adventure-world of earlier Stevenson, but distance from home is ceasing to equate with the glamour of romance, a tendency which will be even more obvious in the final tales of the South Seas.

'THE BEACH OF FALESÁ' (WRITTEN 1890–1)

Stevenson's years in the South Seas stimulated him in two, perhaps predictable, ways: he wrote about the new world in which he found himself, and he responded afresh to the old Scottish world which never ceased to inform him. Two Scottish works stand out from those he started writing in Samoa: *Catriona* is a substantial achievement and *Weir of Hermiston,* even unfinished, is a notable (if unintended) conclusion to his life's work. Among his stories about the South Seas, on the other hand, it is two shorter works which emerge most powerfully, *The Ebb-Tide* and 'The Beach of Falesá'. In them, we find Stevenson creating fiction out of his full response to the Pacific world he had entered, with its exotic appeal, its social, cultural, political, economic, and racial tensions and diversity, its natural scene, its humanity. On the face of it, he had entered at last that landscape of adventure which he had imagined and written about so successfully a few years earlier – but found, instead, its reality to be even more fascinating than its romantic colour. Indeed, it is in these last works, above all, that the polarities of romance and realism come into particularly sharp focus and he treats these exotic Pacific circumstances with a firm and detailed honesty which has led to comparisons with Conrad.

'The Beach of Falesá' first appeared in book form, following its initial publication in the *Illustrated London News*, in a small collection called *Island Nights' Entertainments* (1893). It was accompanied by two short stories, 'The Bottle Imp' and 'The Isle of Voices'. These last were Stevenson's attempt to write for (rather than, simply, about) the indigenous islanders whose world he had entered: they adopt a new 'voice', that of the traditional island storyteller, and it was these which made his island name 'Tusitala' (teller of tales) appropriate and seemingly natural in Samoa. They are very different from the rest of his work, and certainly look a little odd, despite their shared geography, when juxtaposed with 'The Beach of Falesá'. Stevenson did not want the two kinds of story published together: as he wrote to Charles Baxter (11 August 1892), 'The B. of F. is *simply not* to appear along with 'The Bottle Imp', a story of a totally different scope and intention, to which I have already made one fellow, and which I design for a substantial volume' (Mehew 501). Distance, however, and the determination of the publisher meant that this preference was disregarded. Modern readers are likely to find the two short stories to be pleasant curiosities which do not greatly alter our estimation of Stevenson one way or the other. That said, when Arthur Quiller-Couch reviewed the collection in the journal *Speaker*, he unhesitatingly pronounced 'The Bottle Imp' the best work of the three (Maixner 413). The two shorter stories are an outsider's attempt at highly localized South Sea folk-tales, for all the European familiarity of the narrative elements of each: 'The Bottle Imp' tells of a compact with the Devil, and of the requirement to lose the bottle of the title by selling it ever more cheaply before one ends up in Hell; 'The Isle of Voices' features miraculous transportation by means of (yes) a magic carpet. In both tales the supernatural is real and to be believed in, as Samoan culture insisted, and they are excellent illustrations of Stevenson's constant willingness to respond to fresh and highly diverse inspiration.

In 'The Beach of Falesá', however, the islanders' beliefs are viewed from the point of view of the somewhat less superstitious Europeans, although the psychological (and, indeed, economic) realities of superstition are clearly understood. Stevenson treats the islanders' mentalities with the same acceptance and sensitive appreciation as he does the physical environment: this is simply the Samoan world which incomers must live in. They have made their choice, like Stevenson himself. Of course, many of the European characters made that choice for gain and are there as exploiters; some, however, are washed up, pathetic specimens, destroyed physically and spiritually by the very attractions – an environment and a people apparently simply waiting to be carelessly and unscrupulously exploited, a life of cheap comfort and ease, far from the demands and strictures of nineteenth-century Europe – which had made the islands seem so desirable. In comparison with them, the islanders seem, if not noble or savage, at least practical and down to earth. It is the observation of these racial and cultural differences, fundamental to the story, which encourages us to read it as part of the literature, and critique, of colonialism.

The recent emergence of colonial issues into literary prominence, as part of our more widespread reappraisal of the whole history of empire, has helped raise the status of 'The Beach of Falesá'. It certainly offers a critical, totally unflattering picture of the European presence in the South Seas: all the white (male) characters, apart from the missionary, combine greed with a sense of racial superiority. The seediness, cynicism, and drunkenness, which is the default condition of the European traders, is quickly summed up for the hero Wiltshire, and for us, by the captain who transports him to Falesá and who helpfully sketches the community in which his passenger is about to settle. Despite Stevenson's honesty about the physical and moral squalor of the European inhabitants of Falesá, however, the story lacks the edge of anger and deep repulsion which one feels in *Heart of Darkness*, with which it is sometimes compared. There is no horror to compare with the grove of the dying which Marlow discovers at the river station – indeed, nothing to compare with the complex and diverse horrors which Conrad's story unfolds even before Kurtz's famous cry. Stevenson's trader Case is gradually revealed as having a depth of unscrupulousness and Machiavellianism which intrigues the reader, but the comparison is surely not with Conrad's famous European renegade but with Stevenson's own James Durie? That said, the honesty, detail, and commitment to realism which mark the tale necessarily create a totally unflattering account of the European presence in the region, an account which must be regarded as one of the English language's major literary treatments of empire.

As one would expect, recent criticism reflects awareness of the importance of colonial issues in Stevenson's final phase and, indeed, Ann C. Colley has written a valuable book on the whole subject.[9] Similarly penetrating is an essay by Sylvie Largeaud-Ortega which offers us a Stevenson so well informed about South Sea culture that these late writings carry impressive anthropological weight.[10] She sees a positive didacticism in 'The Beach of Falesá' and reads it not solely as a tale which acknowledges the selfish destructiveness of the European presence in the region but also as one which sketches and reflects the mysterious (to Europeans) complexities of South Seas culture. In her reading, its heroine Uma is providing her husband not only with a sexual and family life but also with a rootedness and cultural stability he had never known as a sailor until he settles into the initially alien way of living and thinking.

Two key moments which focus Stevenson's consciousness of the moral dubiety of colonialism are neither of them as penetrating nor as grandly weighty as Conrad's vision, yet they are memorable enough: the infamous marriage contract, and the masterly final lines of the story. It is the peculiar mark of Stevenson's subtle genius that at first glance these seem to belong merely to the comedy of Wiltshire's journey to domestic contentment; they are very far from the grotesquely powerful imaginings of *Heart of Darkness*. Between them, they mark for the reader the beginning and the final stage of Wiltshire's involvement with Uma, the relationship which is at the heart of the tale. These two moments lay bare, however, different but related aspects of the attitudes of white incomers to the native women they encounter; they encapsulate the racial and sexual dimensions of the colonial situation, at that time and in that place, as a whole, and one realizes the boldness of Stevenson in confronting all this. The infamous fake marriage certificate, by means of which Uma is tricked into believing she is properly married to Wiltshire, caused alarm and shock in the late Victorian literary world, for it makes breezily explicit the free sexual use of the local women habitual to the European incomers: 'This is to certify that *Uma* daughter of *Fa'avao* of Falesá island of —————, is illegally married to *Mr John Wiltshire* for one night, and Mr John Wiltshire is at liberty to send her to hell next morning.'[11] This was variously censored in the earliest printings of the story, although, strangely enough, an equal explicitness (using the same key phrases) in the account Stevenson wrote about sex and marriage in the Gilbert Islands in his travel book *In the South Seas* seems to have caused little comment. In formulating this document, Case naturally assumes that one night of sex with Uma will be all that Wiltshire will require, a single night with the taboo-cursed girl being enough (we eventually discover) to scare off the community from dealing with the new trading rival who has just stepped on shore. We share with Wiltshire his first glimpse of Uma: pure sex object in her clinging wet chemise. And his careless choice of her as bed-partner ('Who's she?' said I. 'She'll do.' (BF 7)) does not suggest any higher, or more subtle, response on his part. Yet hints of the fuller and deeper relationship with her, which will gradually emerge, are already there in his instant perception of her 'shy, strange, blindish look, between a cat's and a baby's' and in his surprisingly heated response to the suggestion that she can be bought as cheaply as any other native girl: 'I suppose it was the smile stuck in my memory, for I spoke back sharp. "She doesn't look that sort," I cried.' (BF 7) Stevenson's original conception of the scene was even more rich and complicated, however, as Barry Menikoff has revealed. Stevenson first wrote 'sly', not 'shy': the change of letter altered Uma from a knowing, sexually forward little minx to a sweet, vulnerable damsel more acceptable to the European readership, in the estimation of Colvin and the publisher.[12]

From these unpromising beginnings, the relationship between Wiltshire and Uma grows, each responding instinctively to what is good and lovable in the other. After the dangerous adventure of their final combat with Case, they settle into a life of married contentment; Wiltshire had been morally outraged by the trick played on the girl at the outset, and marries her properly when he gets the chance. So by the end, as he narrates the tale, they have reached a settled phase of middle-aged domesticity. However, a further aspect of family life is now on Wiltshire's mind, and Stevenson brings into sharp focus, once again, the tension between Wiltshire's instinctive goodness and capacity for love, and his continuing entrapment in the unshakeable prejudices of his race and age:

> I'm stuck here, I fancy. I don't like to leave the kids, you see: and – there's no use talking – they're better here than what they would be in a white man's country, though Ben took the eldest up to Auckland, where he's being schooled with the best. But what bothers me is the girls. They're only half-castes, of course; I know that as well as you do, and there's nobody thinks less of half-castes than I do; but they're mine, and about all I've got. I can't reconcile my mind to their taking up with Kanakas, and I'd like to know where I'm to find the whites? (BF 71)

A father's natural love comes into unresolvable conflict with the prejudices which lie within and around him. Thus, Stevenson avoids allowing the adventure-story strand of the tale, which reaches its climax in the explosion and the deadly scuffle, to lead unthinkingly into a happy-ever-after ending. Arthur Quiller-Couch lost interest in the story, he claimed, at the point where it becomes clear, with the real marriage to Uma, that it is Wiltshire's better self which has finally prevailed. For the moral-minded Victorian, that would have been conclusion enough. Stevenson, however, gives us more: he shows this marriage of miscegenation being cemented not just by sex, nor simply by Uma's instinctive desire to build a marriage home, nor by Wiltshire's not quite buried decency, but by the intensity of feeling – feelings of love and respect, brought to the surface by the presence of danger – which the adventure episode generates. The love between the two is, as it were, fired and hardened by Case's attempt at double murder.

For Stevenson is aware that in a situation like that of Samoa, differences of race and culture can combine with the passage of time to take its toll on a marriage. The original physical appeal of Uma, so regularly touched upon through the story, has given way to something less dreamlike and libido-stirring: the devil-girl lookalike has become 'the old lady...She's turned a powerful big woman now, and could throw a London bobby over her shoulder.' (BF 70) It seems that it is 'the kids' who finally keep him in the South Seas and the telling phrase 'I don't like to leave the kids' seems to suggest that (so far as white people like Wiltshire and his reader are concerned) abandoning them is still an acceptable option which remains open to him – just as, once upon a time, taking advantage of Uma 'for one night' was an option which most whites would presumably have taken. Wiltshire is still the same European trader, despite his progress, we first met. It is one of the story's major triumphs that Stevenson has been able to tell such a morally nuanced story through the first-person medium of this imperfect character.

As he was writing the story, Stevenson admitted to Colvin excitedly, that it was 'so wilful, so steep, so silly – it's a hallucination I have outlived', yet he was extremely pleased with it, partly because it is (as he wrote) 'extraordinarily *true*: it's sixteen pages of the South Seas: their essence' (6 September 1891; Mehew 464). He realized that he was producing something new, a fictional treatment of the South Seas which was showing what the region was really like, in contrast to the romanticized versions which had appeared hitherto.

> It is the first realistic South Sea story; I mean the real South Sea character and details of life; everybody else who has tried, that I have seen, got carried away by the romance and ended in a kind of sugar candy sham epic, and the whole effect was lost – there was no etching, no human grin, consequently no conviction. Now I have got the smell and look of the thing a good deal. You will know more about the South Sea after you have read my little tale, than if you had read a library. (24 September 1891; Mehew 467–8)

Few readers are likely to dispute this, nor, I think, are they likely to regret that, as the tale progresses, documentary realism is somewhat nudged aside by romantic adventure: Wiltshire penetrates the secret of the forest, and puts an end to Case's hold over himself and the rest of the island community. The retreat from the familiar and communal, to a separate domain where oppressive evil can be finally dealt with, is a pattern which Stevenson here repeats from *The Master of Ballantrae*. Wiltshire's journey to Case's 'temple' may not be so distant, or so epic, as the upstate winter trek of the Durie brothers, but it allows the same shift to a romantic resolution as we find in the grander novel.

And just as the ending of *The Master of Ballantrae*, however 'steep' and regrettable it may seem to some readers, was part of the original germ of that novel in Stevenson's imagination, so the forest ending of 'The Beach of Falesá' was, in a sense, tied in with the spark of that story. Here is Stevenson's account to Colvin, describing the forest surroundings of his new island home:

> My long silent contests in the forest have had a strange effect on me. The unconcealed vitality of these vegetables, their exuberant number and strength, the attempts...of lianas to enwrap and capture the intruder, the awful silence; the knowledge that all my efforts are only like the performance of an actor, the thing of a moment, and the wood will silently and swiftly heal them up with fresh effervescence; the cunning sense of the *tuitui*, suffering itself to be touched with wind-swayed grasses and not minding – but let the grass be moved by a man, and it shuts up; the whole silent battle, murder and slow death of the contending forest – weighs upon the imagination. My poem 'The Woodman' stands; but I have taken refuge in a new story, which just shot through me like a bullet in one of my moments of awe, alone in that tragic jungle. (3 November 1890; Mehew 440)

At first, the 'new story' was to be called 'The High Woods of Ulufanua'. It was the experience of the Samoan forest which first stimulated Stevenson. 'The contending forest' – the unexpected phrase is fully explored in the poem mentioned here. In 'The Woodman', Stevenson spells out his sense of life's instinctive competitiveness, the universal Darwinian urge to survive and prosper.

> I saw the wood for what it was:
> The lost and the victorious cause,
> The deadly battle pitched in line,
> Saw silent weapons cross and shine:
> Silent defeat, silent assault,
> A battle and a burial vault.
>
> Thick round me in the teeming mud
> Briar and fern strove to the blood:
> The hooked liana in his gin
> Noosed his reluctant neighbours in:
> There the green murderer throve and spread,
> Upon his smothering victims fed,

111

> And wantoned on his climbing coil.
> Contending roots fought for the soil
> Like frightened demons: with despair
> Competing branches pushed for air.[13]

Nor, in this vision, is the conflict simply a peculiarity of the forest jungle: Stevenson contemplates how competition, and the thoughtless destruction of loser by victor, pervades all human interaction and the lives of species:

> The rose on roses feeds; the lark
> On larks. The sedentary clerk
> All morning with a diligent pen
> Murders the babes of other men;
> And like the beasts of wood and park,
> Protects his whelps, defends his den.

> Unshamed the narrow aim I hold;
> I feed my sheep, patrol my fold;
> Breathe war on wolves and rival flocks... (p. 198)

It is an extraordinary vision of deadly individualism and competitiveness, brought on by exposure to the dense jungles of the tropics. And it is from this source, with its unexpected associations, that 'The Beach of Falesá' sprang, by Stevenson's own account. With this in mind, it is scarcely surprising that the tale concludes, not merely with the sentimental union of wronged maiden and good-hearted jack tar, but with a struggle to the death in the darkness of the 'contending forest'. With Case out of the way, and his contrived superstitions swept aside, Wiltshire can describe how his trading in copra could take off at last, and his family life thrive. He can now protect his whelps (problematic as their mixed race makes them) and defend his den. Quiller-Couch missed the point: the union with Uma is not the end of the story Stevenson conceived, but the necessary precondition of a deadly competition in life's jungle which, when won, brings its own rewards.

WEIR OF HERMISTON (WRITTEN 1892–)

This novel is one of various works which Stevenson left incomplete. Most of these are too brief to claim space here, although *St Ives* was nearly finished – indeed, sufficiently advanced to tempt both Arthur Quiller-Couch and Jenni Calder to devise completions. By general consent, however, *St Ives* was never going to be one of Stevenson's best works, unlike the far shorter fragment of *Weir of Hermiston* which, at around 40,000 words, is nevertheless substantial enough to satisfy the reader almost as totally as a completed novel would have done. Furthermore, for *Weir* we have an account of the intended completion, because Stevenson's stepdaughter Belle had been acting as his amanuensis since he became troubled by writer's cramp in 1892 and was in a position to claim to know how the story was to develop further.[14] Apparently, it would have been a tale of full-blown melodrama, with the murder of Frank Innes (as half-promised in the initial 'Introductory' paragraphs), the trial and condemnation of Archie by his father the Lord Justice-Clerk, a movie-style jail-break which would have rescued Archie in the nick of time so that he and his beloved Kirstie could begin life anew in America, and the death of Archie's father as a result of the emotional strain involved in condemning his son to death. The high colour (amounting almost to luridness) of all this would have been in marked contrast to the portion we possess, and while few readers would admit to being glad that Stevenson died when he did, it has been an understandable suspicion that the remainder of the book might not have been so impressively achieved as what we have. As it stands, its eight and a half chapters offer a sure pace and a general psychological fullness, with two figures in particular (Lord Hermiston himself and the elder Kirstie) already so memorably drawn as to rank alongside Stevenson's other best-known characters. In addition, there is a marked wit and vitality in the writing, and a strong sense of structure which confirms Stevenson's confidence in where he was taking his story. One can readily feel how fully Stevenson's heart was in it as he wrote.

Nevertheless, its reputation as Stevenson's masterpiece is no longer accepted unthinkingly. The belief that here, at last, was the undeniably great novel which Stevenson had not hitherto produced was encouraged, if anything, by its unfinished nature: the intervention of death at a moment of apparently supreme achievement can prompt, as in the cases of other unfinished works of art, a certain sentimentality. It is true that Stevenson himself, in a letter written to Charles Baxter almost two years to the day before he died, claimed that 'I expect "The Justice-Clerk" [the then title of the planned book] to be my masterpiece' (1 December 1892; Maixner 464). And so it was proclaimed, by Colvin in particular, when it was published after Stevenson's death. Almost simultaneously, however, doubts were also being expressed, by Quiller-Couch among others, although all regarded it as further clear evidence (if any were needed) of the talent the world had suddenly lost. But was it really going to be the masterpiece with which Stevenson would finally fully match the achievements of illustrious predecessors? There have always been doubts. A similar pattern of critical panegyric followed by gently expressed demurrals was initiated for a later generation by David Daiches's account and assessment of the book, which is the culmination of his short but crucial study of 1947.[15] It feels hard to disagree with his description of it as 'both the most mature and the most perfect thing Stevenson ever wrote' (p. 140), but at the same time one can sympathize with Frank McLynn when he says that '*Weir of Hermiston* does not grab by the throat as *The Master of Ballantrae*, *The Beach of Falesá*, and *Kidnapped* do'.[16] Daiches and McLynn are looking for different things from Stevenson: Daiches for an adult emotional and psychological maturity such as one finds in (say) George Eliot, McLynn for a narrative and imaginative vigour which might often be best found in more popular writing. You pays your money... It is true that it can be difficult, while reading *Weir*, to feel totally carried away by narrative momentum, if only because the heart of the story is only slowly getting under way by the end of the fragment; what we have is all, essentially, preparatory. Nevertheless, it is a marvellous creation of character, style, atmosphere, historical depth, and authorial engagement; it fully displays so many of Stevenson's strengths as a writer.

That his engagement is to be felt so readily in the writing on every page can be related to at least two major concerns which clearly fed Stevenson's imagination while writing the book: they are obvious, and are regularly mentioned by critics. A now far-distant Scotland, with the inevitable recollections of his own earlier days there, was clearly vivid in his mind; and here also was Stevenson's most direct and powerful fictional treatment of the tension between father and son, a concern which can be perceived easily in many of his earlier works and which dominates many recent accounts of his life. Not that the primary interest of the tale lies in its intimations of Stevenson's psychology: once again, whatever may have been his emotions during his years in Samoa, Stevenson is taking the material of his own life experience to develop a work of art which requires no autobiographical connection to engage our attention. His knowledge of Edinburgh, and of the law (however happily abandoned by his student self), his love of Scottish landscape, of balladry, and indeed of Scott – all come into focus through his sense of history, which enables his tale to be both distanced and immediate. His own life gave him insight into the conflict between generations; Scotland's (and, particularly, Edinburgh's) history gave him Braxfield.

As is well known, Adam Weir of Hermiston was modelled on one of the most famous of all Scottish judges, Robert Macqueen, Lord Braxfield (1722–99), noted for his insistence upon speaking Scots on the bench when his fellow judges had adopted polite English. He was equally noted for his vigour in condemning any traces of sedition which appeared before him during the years of vicious conservative reaction against the revolutionary impulses emanating both from France and from the home-grown injustices generated within late eighteenth-century Britain. Stevenson (like all informed citizens of nineteenth-century Edinburgh) was fully familiar with Braxfield's public reputation and had responded powerfully to Raeburn's great portrait of him, as we can see in *Virginibus Puerisque*. In the novel, therefore, he has taken this public possession – the 'image' of the monster Braxfield – and imagined it in terms of private family life so that it acquires a new energy and, more importantly, a humanity and complexity for which the Braxfield legend had no room. Stevenson achieved this, as is equally widely acknowledged, by making the relationship between the two Weirs a reflection of that between the two Stevensons — or at least a version of what Louis had often felt about his relationship with his father. Consequently, this reworking of the legend of the terrible Braxfield finds room for qualities to be respected, and even liked: Adam Weir's combination of high intelligence and total emotional clumsiness, his doggedness in climbing 'the great, bare staircase of his duty, uncheered and undepressed' (XIV, *WH* 25), the unflinching sturdiness of his individuality both in his public and private lives, the glimpsed capacities for love and for an emotional life which family circumstances fail to give him (a lack due as much to the failings of wife and son, as to his own personality), his wisdom in his judgements both on the bench and in his dealings with his son. His unyielding individuality is even capable of giving rise to humour, as he responds to the inadequacy of his wife's house-keeping and as he judges and directs his foolish son in their climactic interview. Indeed, like Falstaff, he is capable of arousing humour in others, as when Lord Glenalmond steers Archie towards a better understanding of his father, and when his author allows us to glimpse Weir's wooing technique ('Haangit, mem, haangit' (*WH* 7)). The near-comic exchange between Weir and Kirstie as she announces the sudden death of his wife is one of the richest passages in the whole book.

Braxfield's personality and behaviour was one of many local legends in a city which was full of them by the late Victorian period: Adam Weir's creator would soon become another one himself. Stevenson knew that many of his readers in Scotland would know his source for this character, and appreciate the use he was making of it. Adam Weir is not the historical Braxfield, who died several years before the period of the story, but he is obviously a version of the real judge, nevertheless. He neatly embodies Stevenson's whole approach to the use of history in his fiction, which involves locating his narratives between the apparently solid 'actuality' of novelistic realism and the far more free, less precise 'history' of legend and folk-memory. His method is thus different from Scott's, whose scholarly history in his novels is strikingly detailed and apparently reliable – except, of course, when he freely invents historical events, or boldly bends the facts of history, for the larger sake of his novel and its meaning. Stevenson, on the other hand, constantly evokes, though lightly and generally, historical circumstances without implicitly insisting on enlightening his reader in a sustained history lesson, as Scott constantly does. It is as if Stevenson is confident that his reader knows enough about the novel's historical setting to make Scott's pedagogy largely unnecessary: a story like *Weir of Hermiston* is set in a time and place with which (he appears to be assuming) both author and reader are broadly familiar. So, where Scott implicitly writes so as to impart some of his own vast knowledge, Stevenson writes to include his reader in a communal possession. In his hands, history becomes folk-memory and legend, a possession of the community rather than of the solitary specialist. The 'Introductory' paragraphs are explicit about this and about his sense of writing 'a Border story' (as he puts it later while telling of the Four Black Brothers) – the border region is one of Scotland's richest sources of ballads and was steeped in folk-memory. The fictional particularity with which a novel normally deals has become transformed, we are told here at the outset, into an imaginative construct larger than life, simpler, more powerful, and more primitive: 'the facts of the story itself, like the bones of a giant buried there and half dug up, survived, naked and imperfect, in the memory of the scattered neighbours'. Edward Cowan has pointed out how that apparently unimpeachable historical novel, *Kidnapped*, is actually 'a romance in which History seldom intrudes yet is ever present, a novel of landscape', while *The Master of Ballantrae*, apparently just as historical and geographical, is specific and informative about neither subject.[17] Stevenson offers, characteristically, the sensation of real-life particularity while actually creating a fictional space of his own invention (*Treasure Island* provides us with a detailed map, but could anyone locate it on 'the' map? *Jekyll and Hyde* is apparently set in London, but many readers 'feel' it in Edinburgh. And so on.) It is part of Stevenson's particular genius that his writing characteristically locates itself comfortably between an actual world and the world formed by, and existing within, the imagination. A *sensation* of place and time is always conjured up in his writing, but there is often a lack of the specific detail which would embed each fictional 'world' in a historical reality. Voices in the dark: the speech and actions of characters are the consistent focus.

In *Weir of Hermiston*, the relationship between a 'historical' reality and the reality pictured by legend works in both directions, and looks as if it was to have been a major preoccupation of the completed novel. The 'Introductory' faces both ways, promising 'the facts of the story itself' but obtaining them from local memory (rather than anything better docu-mented) and also suggesting that they will retain the legendary aura they have acquired. Furthermore, the tale will be centred, it would seem, on a particular spot already steeped in folk-memory and the bloody violence of the past: here already, history has become legend – but legend has kept history alive, however imperfectly. Stevenson's tale, one assumes, will aspire to the status of the 'monument with some verses half defaced', an attempt to fix historical facts which will morph into something more quaint, mysterious, and legendary. Similarly, as we have seen, Adam Weir's origins in Braxfield ground him in both history and Edinburgh's folk-memory.

Stevenson, with his predilection for the romance process of making a selection from the myriad details of life in order to produce art of 'significance or charm' (letter to Bob Stevenson, 30 September 1883; Mehew 234), might be expected to be wholly in favour of the reductive, simplifying, imaginatively powerful vision of balladry and folk-memory, but when Mrs Weir focuses her vision of life through just such a mode of understanding (in her case, the folk-tales of seventeenth-century religious persecu-tion), the result is clear inadequacy. 'Her view of history was wholly artless, a design in snow and ink' (*WH* 11): it is a sensibility at odds with the reality of living, and it is ironic that it is only at the very end of her life that she is able to move on from its stark simplicities to begin to comprehend the complexity and contradictoriness of her husband: 'Mr Weir isna speeritually minded, but he has been a good man to me.' (*WH* 18) In the completed portion of the novel which we possess, this is also the essential tale which is told of Archie Weir: he moves from his maternally induced simplicity of vision (with particular applica-tion to his father) to a more complex, fair-minded, and (we are encouraged to believe) true perception of him. Real life and real people are complicated; simple moralities are inadequate, as Archie is beginning to realize. Account must be taken of this complexity so that adequate judgements can be made. Both outlooks are within him, however: he is as double as any other Stevenson character, torn as he is between his instinctive attraction to designs in snow and ink and his developing appreciation of the complexities and messiness of human realities. (Stevenson's awareness of this contradiction also emerges in his treatment of the law here: Hermiston's firm clarity of judgement on the bench is admirable and necessary, but it inevitably fails to acknowledge the finer details of the lives of human beings – as poor Duncan Jopp discovers.) What we shall never experience, of course, is the drama of this inner conflict when the major crisis of Archie's life – the love tangle which will kill Frank Innes – comes to a head.

If confirmation be needed of Stevenson's concern with these alternative ways of viewing the world, it is surely provided by the tale of the Four Black Brothers (as they are known in the area around Hermiston). They belong to both worlds, that of history, progress, and the just judging of men and their behaviour , and that of legend, primitive violence, and the swift unleashing of passionate action. By the time of Archie's arrival at Hermiston, they are solid, law-abiding members of modern Scottish society, yet in the not-too-distant past (Stevenson dates the event in 1804, lest the episode seem to emerge too completely from a timeless past) they had avenged their father's murder in a spasm of savage justice more characteristic of an earlier epoch still. It would appear that Stevenson's plan for the remainder of the book involved them finding once again that ancient Border vigour and capacity for simple justice – in which case the conflict of the two codes, of legendary action and modern rational judiciousness, would have spanned the whole work. As it is, the tale of their vengeance stands as a challenge to the early nineteenth-century world of the rest of the fragment. Their violent decisiveness in hunting down their father's murderers seems to take even themselves by surprise, revealing a hitherto unsuspected primitive layer in their very beings: their double-ness is not so far from the discovery of Hyde hiding in Jekyll. At one level, the contrast is one of psychology; at another level, it is a matter of alternative narrative modes. In a work which is, despite Stevenson's romance preferences, a modern novel of familiar human motivations and behaviours, he inserts a ballad-tale of astonishing violence and passions.

The contrast and relationship between the worlds of past and present was clearly strong in Stevenson's conception of the work, but its unfinished nature prevents us from saying, simply and securely, that this is what *Weir of Hermiston* is about. Indeed, it is one of the striking features of the book that it can seem to be 'about' so many different things. Its incompleteness means that there is no dominant way of approaching it; the fragment confronts us with a large number of emerging themes and emphases so that numerous interpretations appear to be available. Thus, the contrast of tale-types we have been considering gives rise to various other contrasts, all variations on the theme of past and present. Clearly, the tale of how the four brothers obtained justice for their father contrasts with the approach to justice embodied in the courts of Edinburgh, yet even before they are introduced we have been offered differing concepts of justice in the reaction of Archie to his father's handling of the law. The nature of justice is a prominent thread in the fragment we have, and it was likely to have become ever more so, as Stevenson worked out his tale of murder, trial, and escape. In this matter as in others, however, Stevenson was unlikely to fall into the simple oppositions of Archie's mother: although Adam Weir is a staunch upholder of the criminal law, he also seems to have a kinship with the spirit of the brothers as they hunt down Dickieson and the others. Despite his adherence to the judicial forms, there is a personal, brutal, inhumane, and seemingly vindictive quality in his steering of Duncan Jopp towards the gallows, as Archie finds. A spirit from the past appears to have survived into the supposedly more civilized present.

An understanding of how the past is still relevant to the present is basic to the vision of the book as we have it, as several of the issues already touched upon suggest. One further aspect of this might be mentioned: heredity and inherited psychology are woven into the book's design. On the face of it, it was intended to be the tale of how a gentle, civilized young man committed murder, and thereby continued the history of violence already associated with the Border area. Stevenson's perception of Archie's nature has at least two layers: his psychological inheritance from his parents and, further back, the less tangible but seemingly just as powerful influence of his more distant family and regional past. Stevenson was apparently about to bring the tale of the young people and their amorous triangle to the point at which the apparently submissive and withdrawn young man, opposed to violence, would find within himself the impulse to shoot the betrayer of his beloved. His mother, meek as she was, has already embodied and passed to him a passionate, indeed fanatical, willingness to assert what she deems to be right and true. She adheres to a no-compromise tradition of religious rectitude, one which, in the past, had not been afraid to defend its beliefs with violence. Apparently very different, her husband is an uncompromising upholder of the legal version of justice, but is as willing as his wife's spiritual predecessors to assert righteousness to the point of death: as he says, he is an old man who certainly does believe in capital punishment. The first chapter sets them before us as individuals and as an ill-assorted couple, and also begins to show us how Archie combines their traits. And behind them is the violent history of the family generations on his mother's side: Stevenson clearly relishes for its own sake that history he cheerfully summarizes, but it will play its part in this nineteenth-century story. The violence of the family and regional inheritance will make its contribution to Archie's personality and actions: to an extent, in Archie's case at least, heredity is destiny, and contributes to that air of fatefulness which reinforces the book's ballad atmosphere.

Another aspect of Stevenson's evocation of the ballad is the importance he accords the sense of place in the novel, namely the Scottish Border region as a whole, and a specific spot, the Weaver's Stone. The world of folklore and folk-memory is one in which tales are frequently anchored in specific locations. Folk-memory is a faculty in which history and geography often become one, as Stevenson's own 'Introductory' illustrates. Admittedly, *Weir of Hermiston* is not unusual in making much of location, so far as Stevenson's work is concerned: we have already noted Edward Cowan's description of *Kidnapped* as a novel of landscape, and the prominence of the fictional environment in our experience of each of his major works is notable. Here, however, Stevenson gives this characteristic its head, locating his action in a notably story-rich region. Indeed, one even suspects that when it came to the killing of Frank Innes, there would have been a suggestion that the location itself, a scene of murder already steeped in legendary blood, would have been felt as playing its part in events.

The brothers, however, appear to be intended to do more in the novel beyond releasing ballad action into the modern world. The diversity of their personalities and their modes of living verges on the schematic: it is as if they are meant to symbolize, as a group, the nature of modern Scotland – or at least the common perception of Scotland. Thus, Clem embodies modern Scottish mercantile canniness and commercial growth, Hob the solidity of Scotland's traditional rural life, Gib the nation's strong (and to foreign eyes, eccentric) religious instincts and history, and in Dandie's Burns-like scribblings and amorous escapades Stevenson evokes the freedom and moral-threatening creativity of folk-culture. There is a seemingly formulaic structure to this which suggests a statement about the nation, something encouraged by the juxtaposition of the Enlightenment modernity of Glenalmond's Edinburgh and traditional, rural Hermiston. Who knows? The finished novel may well have offered a statement about Scotland; on the other hand, any novel which makes a feature, however gently, of its regional or national setting is, to some degree, a kind of statement about that setting. Nevertheless, there is a pointed deliberation in the emerging sketch of the nation embodied in this unexpected group of characters which is hard to ignore.

The promised tale of imprisonment and jailbreak seemed likely to draw the work, eventually, into the ambit of Stevenson's earlier adventure romances. Yet the careful unfolding of (in particular) Archie's psychology, and also the complexity and generosity with which Adam Weir himself is created, do indeed suggest that Stevenson was continuing to develop as a writer; certainly, any lingering boy in him, writing for other boys, was growing very small. Readers may also sense a further maturity in the book's treatment of women, and of love, both of which have a subtlety and ambition new to his writing. Stevenson's few previous attempts at portraying young love, in *Prince Otto* and *The Black Arrow*, for example, are not generally counted among his strongest moments. One must also acknowledge, however, that he was constantly aware of being hampered by the prudishness of contemporary taste, especially when he strove in later works to deal honestly with sexuality. While never achieving Lawrence's directness, however, or even Hardy's, he did manage in his final years to write somewhat more openly about sex — and about women, and love, more generally. David Balfour's feelings for, and dealings with, the prominent female characters in *Catriona* arguably succeed where Stevenson's attempts earlier in his career did not. Similarly, the love triangle in *The Master of Ballantrae*, with its evocation of sexual tension, mistrust, and ambiguity, suggests a burgeoning confidence. His South Seas writings were carrying him further still in this direction, and it is notable how central to the design of this novel he now makes the two Kirsties. Of the two, however, it is the elder Kirstie who impresses the reader more: Stevenson's handling of the growing love between Archie and young Kirstie is described with a welcome directness and fullness, but can still seem to be veering towards the sentimental and the formulaic. The elder Kirstie, however, is another matter. We are in no doubt about either her physical charms or her capacity for passion, so that her failure to marry makes her frustration credible and tangible. As a consequence, her feelings towards the young man who suddenly arrives in the household need not be spoken, either by her to herself or by her author to his readers: as often before, Stevenson creates an interpersonal relationship – a situation, focusing on how characters act and communicate, as he explained to Henry James – which speaks largely for itself. When Archie's love for her niece becomes apparent, Kirstie's decisive intervention, which suddenly makes Archie regard his trysting with the caution which will prove tragic, is at least partly the outcome of her jealousy. Nevertheless, we can also sense the woman's deepest feelings about her own missed possibilities, her own tragic subjection to the passing of time.

If the novel, short and fragmentary as it is, nevertheless succeeds in adding a further two memorable characters to those in Stevenson's earlier works, it is distinguished above all for the creative energy we can sense as we read. This is to be found at all levels: the strength of narrative invention, the solidity of Archie's psychological inheritance and the rendering of the family dynamics, the vivid portrayal of Adam Weir and the thoughtful complexity of the emerging judgement upon him, the fecundity of emerging themes and concerns, the confident control of the growing atmosphere of fatefulness, and (on every page) the sheer joyful verve of the writing. It is not only the great set-piece scene, between the chastened Archie and his father, which shows yet again Stevenson's mastery of telling dialogue: many shorter scenes and fragments reveal the same skill. Equally, Stevenson's ability to summarize, with the utmost deftness, whole situations and continuing histories is on full display, as in his accounts of the family at Hermiston, the situation of Archie as he settles into his reclusive exile, the growing tensions between him and Frank Innes in their uncomfortable isolation, and even in the family and regional histories which might have been so dry to read, despite their necessity. The beautifully judged air of comic irony in these accounts is matched by comic touches elsewhere – in some of Adam Weir's asides and in the hints of satire in the loving descriptions of each of the brothers. Such irony distances the Stevensonian narrator from the tale, appropriately enough in this latter-day evocation of the ballad spirit. It also conveys Stevenson's sheer delight in verbal creation — which makes death's sudden interruption of the flow all the more startling.

CATRIONA, ALSO KNOWN AS *DAVID BALFOUR* (WRITTEN 1892)

Catriona, the sequel to *Kidnapped*, has never been as popular, or so well known, as the original tale of David and Alan, and the reasons for this are fairly clear. It is far less obviously a book for young people, despite its depiction of young love, with its inclusion of the strange (to modern eyes, at least) cohabitation of David and Catriona, in Holland. Not that there is anything salacious in that part of the book; quite the contrary – it is the purity of behaviour of the youthful hero which now stretches credulity: 'David Balfour's love affair, that's all correct – might be read out to a mothers' meeting – or a daughters' meeting, and would be thought delicate by a strumpet' (to Colvin, 17 May 1892; Mehew 489). Amorousness apart, the book has far less in the way of open-air adventure than *Kidnapped* and, perhaps most disappointingly of all, it has far less of Alan. If the dominant mode of *Kidnapped* is adventure narrative, the dominant mode of *Catriona* is conversation. To cap it all, the book seems broken-backed, with the narrative goal which had been so insistently pursued from the first page, namely David's attempt to give his evidence in the matter of the Appin murder in order to prove the innocence of James Stewart, suddenly disposed of halfway through. Replacing it is a strand which had seemed merely subsidiary, David's relations with another Jacobite, James More, and his daughter Catriona, a story-line which relocates the action to Holland and France, thereby abandoning the Scottish environments which had seemed an essential part not only of the earlier pages but also of the earlier book. On a first reading, especially, *Catriona* is likely to strike the reader as a queer book altogether. And yet Stevenson, in a letter to George Meredith, said that 'I am sometimes tempted to think [it] is about my best work.' (5 September 1893; Mehew 560)

In what sense, and to what extent, is it a true sequel to *Kidnapped*? Some aspects of continuity are extremely strong. It is a commonplace of criticism of *Kidnapped* that its ending can seem perfunctory, with two important story strands, namely the need to tell of Alan's escape from Scotland and also the question of the consequences of the wrongful arrest of James Stewart, requiring resolution. These two are directly dealt with in the later novel. The likelihood of a sequel had been signalled, of course, in the final paragraph of *Kidnapped*, and *Catriona* opens with an extremely self-conscious piece of narrative continuity with David exiting from the British Linen Bank, at the doors of which he had been left in *Kidnapped*. This makes it perfectly possible to read the two novels as one, as recommended by Sir Arthur Quiller-Couch in his 'First Thoughts on *Catriona*' review in *The Speaker* (Maixner 426). And yet *Catriona* reads like a fresh inspiration, as one might expect thanks to the six intervening years.

It is a more overtly serious work than its predecessor, offering a darker view of human behaviour, especially in the realm of what the novel simply refers to as 'politics'. Writing to Colvin, Stevenson proclaimed, 'politics is a vile and a bungling business. I used to think meanly of the plumber, but how he shines beside the politician!' (1 April 1893; Mehew 534) David is caught in a web of murky motivations, double-dealing, and tribal vengeance. Personal ambition masquerades as loyalty to a cause, and immoral behaviour is justified by what we should now refer to as 'national security'. With the idealism of youth, he expects principle to be the guiding light in public matters and private behaviour alike; what he finds is that even the law of the land is less powerful, less supreme, than it ought to be. Emma Letley, in her introduction to a World Classics edition, relates this vision to Stevenson's own experiences of *realpolitik* in the South Seas, a view which Roslyn Jolly not only confirms but which she goes

125

on to base on a little-discussed episode of Stevenson's career, the series of nine letters he wrote to *The Times* attacking the corrupt political arrangements set up by the Berlin Treaty of 1889.[18] That said, the whole direction of the first part of *Catriona* was implicit in *Kidnapped*: Alan had to be slipped out of the country via the treacherous Lowlands, while James Stewart expected to be victimized as soon as he heard of the murder. It is true, however, that the years between the two books had given Stevenson greater experience to draw upon in his depiction of the ways of those in power.

There are continuities between the books, however. In particular, the motif of kidnapping remains prominent: *Catriona* finally focuses on one particular piece of treachery, namely the attempt of Catriona's father to entrap Alan and so mend his relations with the Hanoverian regime against which he had rebelled. Alan escapes from the attempt directed against him, but David was not so fortunate as to avoid an earlier abduction to the Bass Rock. Kidnapping is not merely a handy plot device here (perhaps encouraged by an exploit of D'Artagnan's in Stevenson's favourite *The Vicomte de Bragelonne*); it encapsulates the way in which fate, and human malevolence, can intervene to divert our progress to the goal instinctively sought by all right-thinking people, namely the secure and contented enjoyment of a life of personal fulfilment and self-respect.

Did *Kidnapped* require a sequel? Although Stevenson, for whom literary craftsmanship was a supreme value, was understandably conscious that his earlier tale had major loose ends, one can scarcely maintain that this flaw has troubled the majority of its readers, especially in their youth. That earlier book, one might claim, has both an inner and an outer tale to tell. The inner tale is that of David's coming into his own despite the surprising interventions of the real world; he completes his circular journey from the House of Shaws back to the same place but with the vital and enriching addition of his friendship with Alan. The outer tale consists of the myriad details of people, landscape, chance, treachery, danger and history which clothe the inner one. The issues of the fate of James of the Glens, and indeed of Alan's need to escape from Scotland, belong to the outer tale; few readers young or old have been greatly concerned with them as they close the book, its true ending achieved. In returning to the world of *Kidnapped*, however, with a view to completing the outer tale, Stevenson had to find a new inner story. He devises one built upon the encounter between youthful ideals and the world's grubby reality, with the special Stevensonian twist which associates that imperfect reality with fatherhood. Catriona has a highly unappealing and untrustworthy father, and David has to work out his relationship with the lawyer-politician, but also emergent father figure, Prestongrange. The conventional tale of a hero's inner growth and his finding of love is made complicated as a result of its assimilation in the (to Stevenson) more immediate issue of parents and children.

David's struggle to achieve justice and safety for James of the Glens is a struggle with history, with Highland culture, and with political realities. It is a struggle with the world in which he finds himself, the world created by the fathers. Part One of the novel tells of his heroic but doomed attempt to impose ideals on a world which is far from ideal, the representatives of which embody the legal and political powers of the Scotland of his time. They are headed by the fatherly Prestongrange, and reflect (at a historical distance) the professional Edinburgh world which Stevenson himself, stage by stage, rejected and escaped from. Here, the tale is of that world's moral compromises, primitive vindictiveness, and lack of idealism. Even the advocate Charles Stewart, thirled to the potentially romantic Jacobite cause and capable of engineering the escape of hunted rebels, acts out of a dogged vestige of clan loyalty from which idealism is largely banished: it is a duty which haunts him rather than a cause which inspires. And when the harsh political Edinburgh world has done its worst, David turns his back on it in order to achieve his purely private destiny. At first sight, it seems strange that Stevenson should extend, and geographically relocate, a very Scottish tale which appears to have reached a natural end with the failure to save James and with the sad conclusion of David's relationship with Prestongrange's daughter. Yet the final scenes set on the Continent, with the blight of the treacherous James More, are a justifiable addition to the whole, revealing how the heart of Stevenson's concern here is the theme of the generations, rather than the story of injustice. It is a novel which clearly invites biographical speculation, but its

127

possible origins in Stevenson's own history and psyche are perhaps of less interest to us than its imaginative strengths.

It is a fine Edinburgh novel, taking its place alongside Scott's *The Heart of Midlothian*, Hogg's *Sinner* and Spark's *The Prime of Miss Jean Brodie*. This is not so much a matter of Stevenson's obvious topographical familiarity with the place (of which there is even more evidence in 'The Misadventures of John Nicholson'). Rather, it is due to Stevenson's total success in conveying the sense of a peculiarly small, tight, oppressive environment. The press of people, and of buildings, in the Old Town of Edinburgh is appropriately projected by this tale of a young man in danger, not knowing whom to trust, secretly carrying the burden of his ideals, hopes, and knowledge. Relevant, too, is the small, enclosed tightness of Edinburgh's social, intellectual, and cultural life – still, perhaps, a feature of the present day, but so much more marked in Stevenson's time and yet more so in the eighteenth century. The sense of an individual closely surrounded by a world from which he is at least partially alienated by what is inside him is one of the principal successes of the book's Part One. This is one of Stevenson's most subtle, but most vivid, evocations of the contrast between public façade and a private, unique, reality. Stevenson knew Edinburgh as well as anyone, of course, and needed no literary model to enable him to recreate the friction between it and a passionate and sensitive individual. Nevertheless, it seems appropriate to wonder how far he was also drawing on the eighteenth-century Edinburgh evoked so vividly in the poems of Robert Fergusson, with whom he felt such an intense identification (Mehew 581–2). That Stevenson would have had a general awareness of them, as he wrote *Catriona*, seems likely enough but one's suspicions are strengthened when one notes that as part of his rendering of life in an upper-class household of 1751 he makes Prestongrange's eldest daughter turn to the harpsichord to entertain David 'with playing and singing, both in the Scots and in the Italian manners' (VI, C. 47). The co-presence of traditional Scottish music with the new, fashionable taste for Italianate styles and forms is an issue – it was felt by Fergusson and his contemporaries to be an issue – which recurs in Fergusson's poems.

Above all, however, it is in the vitality of the conversations which abound in the book that one senses Stevenson's experience of social life amongst Edinburgh's professional classes. Voices in the dark? His ability to invent dialogue which crackles with life, drama, and significance had been visible in earlier works, of course – not least in *Kidnapped* where the verbal exchanges between Alan and Robin Oig, between Alan (again) and Uncle Ebenezer at the book's conclusion, and between (above all) Alan and David in the great quarrel scene are among the work's highlights. *Catriona*, however, has a notable abundance of such, to the extent that they begin to seem the book's basic medium. In the earlier book, too, Alan had often seemed an essential element of these exchanges; it is one of the ways in which Stevenson suggests David's growing confidence and maturity – and his right to his place as the book's hero – that he is the one whose force and vigour so animates the verbal tussles in the later novel. This argumentative David is a David we have not seen before; his Whiggism stands positively on its own, rather than emerging as previously in contrast to Alan Breck Stewart's Jacobitism. Stevenson's conception of the story, of course, demands that David, determined to pursue a course of action from which so many try to dissuade him, be involved in any number of pointed arguments. Imagining these, however, is clearly no chore for the author, with his palpable delight in inventing those scenes, not least the one in Chapter 17 in which James Stewart's defence lawyers greedily contemplate the prospect of the opportunities which would arise from the defeat of Prestongrange and the Duke of Argyle, the two law officers leading the prosecution of their client.

Embedded in the novel is one of Stevenson's fine short stories: 'The Tale of Tod Lapraik', the writing of which was clearly an equal pleasure. This is often coupled in the minds of readers with 'Thrawn Janet', as it draws on the same world of Scottish history, religion, and folk superstition as that earlier success. It is also, like 'Thrawn Janet', in excellent Scots. It serves the obvious structural function of helping create, for the reader, a sense of David's lengthy period of total passivity on the Bass Rock, completely removed from the flow of events with which he has been engaged. For a spell, he and we are transported to a temporary alternative world. To Stevenson, both the folk-tale nature of the story and the real-life historical associations of the Bass are relevant in achieving this effect. It conjures a world of the yet more distant past, redolent of the passions and conflicts of an earlier time, a primitive era of Highland turmoil and injustice the last vestiges of which are about to slay James of the Glens and against which David's modern Whiggism is struggling. And the sojourn is part of a pattern. *Catriona* removes David twice from its principal Edinburgh location: once to the Bass Rock, embodying a Scotland still in the clutches of the past, and later to Holland and France, where those ancient conflicts are finally put to rest and David finds his future at last.

If *Catriona*'s wealth of conversations is a success, so is the major new character of Prestongrange. Alan's role is necessarily diminished in the story the author has chosen to tell, and Stevenson perhaps felt the need of a figure, at David's young shoulder, with some of the same moral ambiguity and experience of the world. Where, in *Kidnapped*, the young David required a senior and knowing guide to make his survival in the wilds of the western Highlands credible, so he now needs another such figure to partially explain his survival in the yet more murky dangers to which he commits himself in political Edinburgh. It is easy to categorize Prestongrange as yet another instance of Stevenson's perennial concern with duality: to David, Prestongrange is both a threat and a protector, a figure embodying the impersonal political forces against which he struggles but also a fatherly and apparently sympathetic man who shelters the young idealist from the full rigour of the politically biased law and gives him, recently orphaned, his first taste of a happy domestic existence. If the problem of how far he can be trusted limits David's response to him, it simply makes him all the more intriguing from the reader's point of view. And also from Stevenson's – for the author's imagination is happily at full stretch in devising the fictional circumstances with which the wily schemer entraps David with kindness. In the end, David's resounding judgement brilliantly sums up the delicious dilemma: 'I think shame to write of this man that loaded me with so many goodnesses. He was kind to me as any father, yet I ever thought him as false as a cracked bell.' (C. 183) It is not a judgement which could be applied to either of the two principal female characters, Catriona herself and Prestongrange's elder daughter Barbara. With this novel, Stevenson takes a yet further step towards creating a maturely conceived amorous relationship – a treatment which might convince in a way that love in *Prince Otto* and *The Black Arrow* does not. That David is destined to fall thoroughly in love seems indicated by the early encounter with the lass with the 'wonderful bright eyes' and the parted lips. That Stevenson, however, was still uneasy in the portrayal of an adult, sexualized love relationship seems indicated by his depiction of David in his later dealings with Catriona. Indeed, Stevenson's method here is to express desire through its contorted thwarting in the artificiality of the domestic arrangements of the young people in Holland. They find themselves in a situation in which the world (including the girl's father) is liable to think the worst of them while the point is, of course, that their behaviour is strikingly chaste. It is at this point, in particular, that one feels the force of Alan Sandison's firm view (of both books) that David Balfour, as a character, is a study in immaturity.

But perhaps that is to take too serious a view of the matter, and it is worth considering that at a certain level *Catriona* is a comedy, despite those grotesque corpses hanging in chains which David encounters as he walks to Pilrig in Chapter 3, and despite the unfortunate end of James of the Glens. That cruel fate merges, however, with the larger portrayal of the period's social and judicial world, treated as it is with a cynicism which borders on wry comedy. Comedy lurks, too, in all those conversations conducted at cross purposes and filled with misunderstandings. From the start, it is a tale of two lovers whose road to happiness in each other's arms is beset by the machinations of an older generation – which is as ancient a comic formula as one might find.

THE EBB-TIDE (WRITTEN 1893)

An excellent illustration of the variety of Stevenson's writing is provided by *The Wrecker* and *The Ebb-Tide*. Written and published in close proximity, each reflects Stevenson's perception of the squalid realities of the European presence in the South Seas and his willing acceptance of that as material for his writing. They were both started by his stepson Lloyd Osbourne and largely completed by Stevenson, in part as acts of friendly cooperative support. Indeed, as noted earlier, Wayne Koestenbaum sees *The Ebb-Tide* as particularly clear evidence of a homosexual relationship between Stevenson and Lloyd and, once more, his discussion results in a stimulating and challenging exploration of the text. He views it, nevertheless, as a kind of playful secret game between them, expressing in code their special affection for each other. However that may be, we need not hesitate to think of both works as essentially Stevenson's, for the bulk of the writing – and who knows how much of the revision of Osbourne's original material – was his. Each represents a mature development of Stevenson's boyish taste for treasure islands, for danger, violence and skulduggery on the high seas, and for mysteries. Each, too, can be mined for further psychological evidence of Stevenson's still unresolved difficulties with his father and all that he had represented. And yet, to the modern reader especially, they are chalk and cheese.

Partly, of course, it is that *The Wrecker* is a full-length – indeed, rather long – novel, whereas if *The Ebb-Tide* is a novel at all (it was certainly published on its own, in hard covers) it is a very short one. More crucially, *The Wrecker* rambles as a narrative, and shifts its mood and narrative focus with each changing geographical location, of which there are five: provincial USA, Paris, Edinburgh, the American west coast, and the South Seas. Consequently, the reader can easily feel as if he or she has five different novel fragments to contend with. As we have seen so often, it is one of Stevenson's particular strengths that he derives creative energy from a sense of place, but he can fall prey to the consequent danger of disunity when a work has a notable diversity of locations; *Catriona* might be another example of this, and this is essentially Daiches's charge against *The Master of Ballantrae*. Those earlier masterpieces, *Treasure Island* and *Kidnapped*, are also marked by sharply contrasted locations, but the opening scenes of the Admiral Benbow and the House of Shaws offer meaningful home-country preludes to the landscapes of adventure which form the main bodies of those books. Those vividly realized settings, 'domestic' locations into which adventure and romance are already seeping, form perfect foils to the main actions. No such larger unity prevails in *The Wrecker*.

Nor might one be tempted to regard it as a work with never a word wasted: indeed, it reads as one of the most over-generously worded of Stevenson's large-scale fictions, in which the stylistic judgement and memorable forcefulness of expression which so strongly mark his greatest pieces of writing seem absent. Fortunately, that satisfying precision of expression, so much part of the pleasure of reading Stevenson, would return with the unfinished *Weir of Hermiston*, and is also a welcome feature of *The Ebb-Tide*.

Of the two South Seas novels, however, it was *The Wrecker* which enjoyed the more secure initial success. With all its variety, it is a buoyantly imagined piece of work, sufficiently endowed with quirky, memorable characters and with much to remind Stevenson's legion of eager readers, reassuringly, of past pleasures. Colvin did not care for it, but then he did not care for any of Stevenson's South Seas writings (let alone for the actual decampment to the South Seas); nevertheless, it was a popular and critical success. *The Ebb-Tide*, however, produced much puzzlement and a certain amount of disgust: the unrelenting focus on squalid characters and behaviours seemed dangerously close to Zola's realism rather than to Stevensonian romance, and the general bleakness of outlook seemed equally uncharacter-istic. Stevenson, however, seems to have relished the unattrac-tive-seeming material. In a letter to Colvin (August 1890; Mehew 425), he describes the 'Pearl Fisher' (as he was then calling it) as 'far more important' than *The Wrecker* and sees Lloyd as being 'of course quite incapable of turning the ugliness of this rugged, harsh and really striking tale'. Three years later, in a letter to Henry James (17 June 1893; Mehew 545), he was calling its characters 'such a troop of swine', and recognizing that some readers of the story might think him converted to Zola's school of fiction. He acknowledged that the story's 'ugliness and pessimism' resembled the Frenchman's work, but denied that it had that quality of 'rancidness' which seemed to add to Zola's appeal. Nevertheless, Stevenson found the book strangely hard to write, as he squeezed out small daily portions rather than the pleasurable flow to which he was accustomed. It is now regarded as among his greatest works. Not only does its thorough and honest portrayal of the moral squalor of so much European activity in that part of the world make it an even more telling response to colonialism than 'The Beach of Falesá' (with the inevitable, but appropriate, comparisons with Conrad) but its (at first) strange structure and even stranger ending offer a challenge which modern readers welcome as much as its first readers disliked it. It feels like an extremely modern book, which takes its appropriate place in, for example, Alan Sandison's account of Stevenson and Modernism, and also in Ann C. Colley's recent monograph on Stevenson and colonialism. It engages the reader at a variety of levels, and amounts to a fascinating transformation of some of Stevenson's favourite fictional materials.

It has no hero, either in the sense of a principal character who is worthy and to be identified with, or even in the sense of one who is undoubtedly central. Rather, it is all about the interaction of a group of three down-and-outs with scarcely a remaining finger-hold on morality. Then the three become four, as they encounter someone who claims the highest level of Christian righteousness but who is even more morally dubious, and at least as dangerous, as they. The focus on these groupings (rather than on a central character) is highlighted in the titles of the two parts into which the story is divided: 'The Trio' and 'The Quartette'. Indeed, the musical dimension of these terms seems further suggested by the intertwining strands of the pairings, the alignments, the contrasts and the oppositions amongst the characters which form the essence of the unfolding narrative. (There are several other unexpected musical references in the text, in addition to these titles – to music by Beethoven and Weber, for example.) Stevenson's interest in patterns of interacting characters, and in their interpersonal strivings for alliance and supremacy, had long been central to his most successful works. However, in those tales of youth beginning to find its way in worlds of adult violence and mystery, *Treasure Island* and *Kidnapped*, the dynamic interactions of Jim Hawkins and David Balfour with those who guide and/or threaten them seem so inevitable as to require no special consideration by the reader. *Jekyll and Hyde* and *The Master of Ballantrae*, on the other hand, give the struggles for dominance between distinctly different (but deeply intertwined) protagonists a central prominence, emphasized in each case by high melodrama and by strong hints of symbolism. Now, in *The Ebb-Tide*, a whole new subtlety emerges in Stevenson's handling of such material, and the interplay of the four characters as they strive to play the hands which chance and their own personalities have dealt them, does indeed begin to resemble a piece of chamber music. In this, Stevenson clearly goes further than ever before: in 'The Beach of Falesá' the 'trio' of Wiltshire, Uma, and Case resolves itself, to a certain extent, into simply a duel (or duet?) between Wiltshire and Case, while the unfinished *Weir of Hermiston* offers merely a sequence of tense pairings: Adam Weir and his wife, Archie and his father, Archie and each of the Kirsties (in turn), Archie and Frank Innes. Perhaps a completed *Weir of Hermiston* would have eventually woven a denser texture out of these dualities, but as things stand it is *The Ebb-Tide*, of all these last works, which (from this point of view at least) foreshadows most interestingly the writings which we never received from the author. While it does indeed seem to hark back to that most famous, and most Stevensonian, tale of South Sea island dangers, it is a work which also seems to hint at a fresh future for his career.

The trio of characters is at its apparently lowest ebb when we first meet them: they are 'on the beach' (in the expressive phrase of that southern time and place), living by begging and sheltering in a deserted jailhouse. Though united in their misfortunes, and in the need for mutual companionship, the three are distinctly delineated. Davis is an American sea-captain guilty of a gross breach of the code of shipboard responsibility (he had lost a ship, and the lives of shipmates, through drink); Huish is 'a vulgar and bad-hearted cockney clerk' (*E-T* 127). Herrick is the university-educated product of a comfortably-off English family, yet his natural advantages in life have been negated by a deep-seated character flaw which has rendered him unemployable in the spheres which should have been his, and he has drifted downwards across continents until washed up on the beach at Tahiti. At the outset, Stevenson's focus on Herrick, combined with the natural class-based assumptions of his readers, seems to mark him out as our main concern, but as the story unfolds our narrow preoccupation with the fate of this one character fades. The tale is of the group as a whole. When chance offers Davis an unexpected command, the trio seem to have started once more on an upward trajectory. Instead,

Stevenson's powerful vision takes them yet further into a despair which neither they nor their readers could have imagined. It is a journey into a strange hopelessness – into an unexpected heart of Stevensonian darkness – as their initial attempts at refreshed rectitude begin to crumble. Davis and Huish rapidly succumb to the temptation of the champagne they carry; they resolve to steal the ship and its cargo but discover that this last, in turn, is worthless and designed as an insurance fraud. In all this, Herrick strives the least feebly to maintain proper (and prudent) conduct. Having crossed the line into major criminality, however, their case is worse than ever: they are totally 'at sea' in a world with no compass (either within themselves or, in actuality, in the oceanic world on which they float) or firmness of character (their very names are suspect). They discover that their limited options are even more limited than they thought: through bad planning and lack of proper shipboard discipline, they are running out of food. Stevenson's confidently paced account of the series of disasters, substantially self-inflicted, leads to a point of hopelessness with no apparent way out.

Chance, however, brings them to an island which, in turn, barely exists either on their charts or in physical actuality: the insubstantial, mirage-like landfall on the horizon is a masterly touch of Stevenson's. No less masterly, however, is the surreal little world they discover there. The island contains an empty-seeming settlement with, as a presiding deity, a great white female figurehead: 'on the top of the beach and hard by the flagstaff, a woman of exorbitant stature and as white as snow was to be seen beckoning with uplifted arm' (E-T 190). Later, from the jungle, strange beings will emerge: 'the sun glistened upon two metallic objects, locomotory like men, and occupying in the economy of these creatures the places of heads – only the heads were faceless. To Davis between wind and water, his mythology appeared to have come alive, and Tophet to be vomiting demons.' (E-T 244) Perhaps strangest of all, the trio will be treated, in this most far-flung spot which hardly exists at all as a reality in the world's awareness, to a gracefully presented dinner in which the forms of polite social intercourse overlay a situation which is as grotesque as it is savage. Herrick has a breakdown as he contemplates the calm murderousness of his host Attwater and he staggers off with Davis trying to calm him: ' "Rather bad form, is it not?" said Attwater. "Well, well, we are left *tête-à-tête*. A glass of wine with you, Mr Whish!" ' (*E-T* 219). The simple reality is that they have stumbled upon an unclaimed and privately occupied island which is being exploited for the pearls in its surrounding waters. It is almost deserted, the greater part of its little population having died in the smallpox epidemic which is sweeping the region. It is presided over by Attwater, the European master of the place, who combines a fervently evangelical Christianity with a ruthlessness backed up by the modern weaponry which he does not hesitate to use. He is a vivid embodiment of the combined forces of Christianity and commercialism which Stevenson saw despoiling the region. The second part of the story, therefore, tells of the inevitable struggle between the trio of bungling thieves who rapidly decide to make their own the treasure of pearls which they know Attwater must possess, and the masterful, if isolated, tyrant who is always in control of the situation. The struggle may be inevitable – its outcome is not. Three of the four characters have no qualms about murder; only Herrick strives to negotiate a less bloody outcome.

The climax comes with a failed murder attempt and a conclusion which confounds expectations – in other words, there is no neatly predictable finality but rather an ending which startles as much as it puzzles. For one thing, Herrick (who, as we have seen, had seemed at the outset to be our main concern) forms no part of the crucial tableau: Huish lies dead, his attempt at an acid attack discovered and foiled by Attwater's skill with a rifle, and Davis, staring down the barrel of Attwater's gun, remains to be dealt with. One is tempted to say that Stevenson employs what a later generation will perhaps think of as the 'Dirty Harry' device: an anecdote earlier in the story seems to indicate what the climax will bring, but the prophecy is turned on its head. Earlier, Attwater had told the tale of how his own skill with a rifle equalled that of an earlier island king who used to 'miss nicely' with every cruel shot, just missing his living target by a hair's breadth, until the last shot 'went plump between the eyes' (*E-T* 209). Now, at the tale's climax, Attwater apparently embarks on the same vicious game and we, with Davis, expect the final shot from the magazine to be an executioner's. Indeed, Davis accepts this imminent death as just, and as ending his hopeless existence appropriately: he utters a prayer commending his two children to God. So instead of slaying him, Attwater comforts him as a penitent whose life has been turned round. The last sentence of the story as Davis pleads with Herrick to 'come to Jesus' – 'I been a sinner myself!' (E-T 252) – is utterly abrupt: even stylistically, one feels that there should be more prose to come. And questions remain: does Davis stay on the island where he has found 'peace in believing'? Indeed, are we to regard Davis's conversion as his final state – and are we to regard the Christianity flowing from Attwater's hands as in itself attractive and desirable? Davis ends the story babbling missionary clichés and Attwater remains the embodiment of the brutal justice which had so outraged Herrick. In Herrick's eyes, Davis is now 'Attwater's spoiled darling and pet penitent'. As for Herrick, he presumably departs with the approaching schooner, and we have little sense that his future will be very different from his past. The high drama of the island adventure has had surprisingly little meaning for him.

If there are a number of questions raised by the ending when looked at one way, when looked at another way, it can seem only too clear. The embarrassing blandishments of Davis's childish attempt at Herrick's conversion ('come to Jesus right away, and let's meet in yon beautiful land' is typical), which ring in our ears as the story's final words, underline how much it has been concerned with religion as a force in the frontier-territory of the South Seas. The two-part structure works simply: the trio of morally bankrupt Europeans destroyed by the challenges of the region are thrown what looks like a lifeline by the miraculous appearance of the island and the religious conviction of its inhabitant. To what extent is Christianity capable of providing these wretches with the spiritual salvation they require? Attwater's religion, it turns out, is flawed both by its capacity for violence and by its involvement in the economic plundering of the region. The Christianity of *The Ebb-Tide* has no capacity to 'save' these people: Huish dies at its hands, Davis is turned into an ineffectual babbler who may never return to the ordinary world of men and women, and Herrick is essentially untouched by it as he departs. It is a hard, dry-eyed examination of the southern world as Stevenson found it to be in 1893.

It offers us no excuse to finally categorize Stevenson as a bleak pessimist, however. There is no hint here that he is summing-up his view of the world of men and women – indeed, there is no 'final' quality about it at all. It simply has its own mood and its own logic. Its abrupt bleakness is merely the implication of the last tale he happened to publish before he died so (one is tempted to say) abruptly.

4

'Under the wide and starry sky'

Stevenson's short poem 'Requiem' is one of the best known and most frequently quoted of his verses but of its eight lines only the first has no reference to death and the grave: read on its own, the line suggests exhilaration, a love of beauty, and openness to the world and to experience. Whereas Stevenson's contemporaries and the immediately succeeding generation saw his early death as a prominent part of his story, today's readers and critics are surely more likely to be conscious of the extent and variety of his highly productive career. Our overriding sense of him as a writer is of brilliance, of copiousness, of the constantly unexpected and of a seemingly natural grace. It is vitality we associate with him, rather than mournfulness – even while we might regret the absence of what further decades could have produced. Stevenson would appear to embody, as well as anybody, the immortality which a great writer can achieve. His reputation among academic critics (to use the simplest phrase) may have died for a while after his death, but it has come back to life again and looks set to remain vital for the foreseeable future. He is now regularly discussed once more as one of the leading authors of his age, whether the critic brings to bear a concern with the historical, social, or psychological circumstances of the period, or is concerned with questions of writerly craft, technique, or theory, or is enlivened by a nationalist point of view. There is a sense, however, in which the scholars and critics are merely catching up with ordinary readers and with other practising writers, who have never ceased to find in Stevenson's works pleasure and high achievement. James Robertson has usefully surveyed the fall and rise of his reputation – a leading Scottish novelist acknowledging a great predecessor.[1]

If Stevenson is now held once more in high regard, there is nevertheless a continuing variability, an unsettled quality, in more particular matters relating to him. For one thing, his life and personality continue to interest equally with his writings. It is as if his reputation as a 'classic' author – based especially, one suspects, on *Treasure Island* and *Jekyll and Hyde* – is a given while his life story, with its family tensions, its religious rebellion, its romantic gestures, the mystery of how finally to interpret and judge the Stevensons' marriage, and the unpredictable boldness of the final home-making on the other side of the world, seems a tale with a vitality of its own. The stream of substantial biographies continues. More than that, it may be that the finished elegance and craftsmanship which so clearly marks his writing, combined with the intensity with which he lived his life, makes him appropriate for deeper psychological specula-tions about his essential personality, such as those of Wayne Koestenbaum and Elaine Showalter, or the (if anything) even more complex reading of his work and personality offered by Hilary J. Beattie.[2]

Furthermore, the question of where, finally, to place him in the competing literary domains he seemed to inhabit – Victorian literature, emerging Modernism, the world of the *belletrist*, children's literature, the debateable lands between realism and romance – continues to tease, although it is that very uncertainty which stimulates so much fruitful discussion and exploration of his works. Current comment offers a welcome variety of focus and approach, whereas those who turned their backs on him in the earlier twentieth century thought they knew what to think of him. One notes, for example, a willingness to compare him ever more frequently with that securely Modernist figure, Joseph Conrad, and not always to Conrad's advantage. Our perception of the links between Stevenson and early Modernism is firming up – Sandison is no longer a lone voice – and this approach helps open up more of Stevenson. Roderick Watson, for example, leads us into works of both fiction and non-fiction in exploring in Stevenson 'a significant anxiety about human agency, ultimate meaning and existence itself', an unease which highlights 'what might be called modernist pre-echoes in Stevenson's work'.[3] It is a fruitful characteristic of current discussion that it is so aware of Stevenson's place in the fascinating conjunction of two eras, late Victorianism and early Modernism. Thus Rosalind Williams can link Stevenson, unexpectedly, with Jules Verne and William Morris as writers who, in their different ways, seemed to be sniffing total change in the world which was emerging.[4]

The present study makes the usual implicit assumption that his supreme achievement, and importance to us, lies in his prose fiction. His other fields of literary activity – verse, essays, memoirs, travel writing, correspondence – have had to take a back seat. Some future all-encompassing critical study which would offer a far more integrated, and so more just, assessment and analysis of his life's work may still be some way off. As it is, one can certainly encourage readers to explore further, assuring them that they are likely to find much pleasure beyond the fiction. As it is, his major collections of poetry have long been enjoyed by many readers, with *A Child's Garden of Verses* (1885) acquiring something of the status of 'children's classic' alongside more widely read works by Lewis Carroll, E. Nesbit, George MacDonald, Kenneth Grahame, and the others. He is invariably represented in anthologies of Scottish verse – and not just by the same poems. On the other hand, he enters the current *Norton Anthology of English Literature* on the strength, simply, of *Jekyll and Hyde*. Harold Bloom perhaps sums up the present assessment of Stevenson's comparative strengths when he describes the heart of Stevenson's achievement as consisting of four works which 'have achieved the status of myth' and which 'seem to have been there even before first he wrote them': *Treasure Island, The Master of Ballantrae, Kidnapped*, and *Jekyll and Hyde*. For Bloom, Stevenson possessed a 'daemonic genius' which 'does not however inform his letters, or his essays and travel-writings. Unfortunately, it is also absent from his poetry, which in consequence is minor though accomplished.'[5] This sums up elegantly a still prevailing view of Stevenson as a whole, though it is worth reiterating that much pleasure is to be had from reading his verse and his letters in particular, the latter especially seeming due for further consideration which could locate Stevenson among the great literary letter-writers.

The same feeling that discriminates between what is really great in Stevenson's fiction itself – arguably, Bloom's four 'mythic' works – and the rest of an extensive, lively, varied but lesser fictional achievement, is what the present work attempts to overcome. While in no way seeking to displace those four from their place in the estimation of the reader, it has seemed worthwhile to make the case for various other works, and to insist that nearly all of Stevenson's stories are very well worth reading. If one had to select other pieces to join the four in their prominence in the critical pantheon, the two great South Seas stories, 'The Beach of Falesá' and *The Ebb-Tide*, are obvious choices, as are the early Scottish tales, 'The Merry Men' and 'Thrawn Janet', though they may require of the reader some familiarity with specifically Scottish perceptions and ways of thinking. *Weir of Hermiston* should be read by everyone with the remotest interest in Stevenson. *New Arabian Nights* and its successor volume present more of a challenge to our preconceptions and our literary receptivity, but in time other writers may follow Alan Sandison's lead and bring about a more general acceptance of their worth. For the moment, however, it is perhaps only necessary to echo Barry Menikoff's stress on how Stevenson's own readers were aware, above all, of his 'versatility and inventiveness': 'It was as if every new book was a surprise.'[6] Present-day readers are likely to find the same.

Notes

CHAPTER 1. INTRODUCTION: *TRAVELS WITH AND WITHOUT A DONKEY*

1. Alistair Fowler, 'Parables of Adventure: The Debatable Novels of Robert Louis Stevenson', in *Nineteenth-Century Scottish Fiction: Critical Essays*, ed. Ian Campbell (Manchester: Carcanet New Press, 1979), 105–29 (106).
2. 'A Gossip on Romance', reprinted in *'The Lantern-Bearers' and Other Essays*, ed. Jeremy Treglown (London: Chatto & Windus, 1988), 172–82 (174).
3. *Travels with a Donkey in the Cevennes*, Skerryvore Edition of the Works of Robert Louis Stevenson (London: Heinemann, 1925), vol. XV, 175. Unless otherwise stated, references to Stevenson's writings are to this edition. The volume number is included with the first page reference to each individual work. For five of Stevenson's works, however, for which Oxford World's Classics or Penguin editions are currently available, references will be made to those rather than to the Skerryvore Edition.
4. Alan Sandison, *Robert Louis Stevenson and the Appearance of Modernism* (Basingstoke & London: Macmillan Press, 1996). Hereafter, quoted as Sandison. Frank McLynn, *Robert Louis Stevenson: A Biography* (London: Hutchinson, 1993). Hereafter, quoted as McLynn.
5. David Daiches, *Robert Louis Stevenson* (Norfolk, Con.: New Directions, 1947). Hereafter, quoted as Daiches. Robert Crawford, *Scotland's Books: The Penguin History of Scottish Literature* (London: Penguin Books, 2007).

CHAPTER 2: 'A BRILLIANT AND ROMANTIC GRACE'

1. Robert Kiely, *Robert Louis Stevenson and the Fiction of Adventure* (Cambridge, Mass.: Harvard University Press, 1965), 114.

2. George Saintsbury, unsigned review in *Pall Mall Gazette*, 4 August 1882, reprinted in Paul Maixner, *Robert Louis Stevenson: The Critical Heritage* (London, Boston & Henley: Routledge & Kegan Paul, 1981), 106–8, 108. Hereafter, reviews quoted from Maixner are indicated in the text itself, thus: (Maixner 108).

3. J. C. Furnas, *Voyage to Windward: The Life of Robert Louis Stevenson* (London: Faber & Faber, 1952), 104.

4. Edwin M. Eigner, *Robert Louis Stevenson and Romantic Tradition* (Princeton: Princeton University Press, 1966), 78.

5. J. R. Hammond, *A Robert Louis Stevenson Companion* (London & Basingstoke: Macmillan, 1984), 74.

6. *Robert Louis Stevenson and the Appearance of Modernism* (Basingstoke & London: Macmillan Press, 1996), 82–144.

7. XVII, 218–19.

8. *Underwoods* (London: Chatto & Windus, 1895), xi–xii.

9. *Selected Letters of Robert Louis Stevenson*, ed. Ernest Mehew (New Haven & London: Yale University Press, 2001), 530. Hereafter quoted as Mehew. Readers are likely to find this selection more accessible than the parent complete edition of Stevenson's letters published by Yale University Press.

10. Henry Thomas Buckle, *On Scotland and the Scotch Intellect*, ed. H. J. Hanham (Chicago and London: University of Chicago Press, 1970), 156.

11. David Daiches, *Robert Louis Stevenson* (Norfolk, Conn.: New Directions, 1947), 29.

12. *Scotland's Books: The Penguin History of Scottish Literature* (London: Penguin Books, 2007), 492–503.

13. Robert Crawford, *Scotland's Books*, 496.

14. *'The Lantern-Bearers' and Other Essays*, ed. Jeremy Treglown (London: Chatto & Windus, 1988), 277–84 (279).

15. Crawford, *Scotland's Books*, 497.

16. *Treasure Island*, ed. Peter Hunt (Oxford: Oxford University Press, 2011), 45. Further references are to this edition.

17. *'The Lantern-Bearers' and Other Essays*, ed. Jeremy Treglown (London: Chatto & Windus, 1988), 282.

18. Alan Riach, *Representing Scotland in Literature, Popular Culture and Iconography* (Basingstoke: Palgrave Macmillan, 2005), 88–100.

19. Oliver S. Buckton, '"Faithful to his map": Profit and Desire in Robert Louis Stevenson's *Treasure Island*', *Journal of Stevenson Studies* 1 (2004), 138–49.

20. Glenda Norquay, *Robert Louis Stevenson and Theories of Reading* (Manchester & New York: Manchester University Press, 2007), 170–9.

21. Julia Reid, *Robert Louis Stevenson, Science, and the Fin de Siècle*

(Basingstoke: Palgrave Macmillan, 2006), 38.

22. Joseph Bristow, *Empire Boys: Adventures in a Man's World* (London: HarperCollins Academic, 1991), 93–126.
23. *'The Lantern-Bearers' and Other Essays*, ed. Treglown, 195.
24. Frank McLynn, *Robert Louis Stevenson: A Biography* (London: Hutchinson, 1993), 222.
25. McLynn, *Robert Louis Stevenson*, 41.
26. *'The Lantern-Bearers' and Other Essays*, ed. Treglown, 195.
27. McLynn, *Robert Louis Stevenson*, 226.
28. Walter Scott, *Waverley*, ed. Claire Lamont (London & New York: Oxford University Press, 1986), 283.

CHAPTER 3: 'SO EASILY THE MASTER OF US ALL'

1. Claire Harman, *Robert Louis Stevenson: A Biography* (London: HarperCollins, 2005), 284–8 (286).
2. Michael Burleigh, *Blood and Rage: A Cultural History of Terrorism* (London: HarperCollins, 2008), 1–18.
3. G. K. Chesterton, *Robert Louis Stevenson* (London: Hodder & Stoughton, 1927), 166–7.
4. Deaglán Ó'Donghaile, 'Conrad, the Stevensons, and the Imagination of Urban Chaos' in Linda Dryden, Stephen Arata, Eric Massie (eds), *Robert Louis Stevenson and Joseph Conrad: Writers of Transition* (Lubbock: Texas Tech University Press, 2009), 159–74.
5. Alan Sandison, *Robert Louis Stevenson and the Appearance of Modernism* (Basingstoke & London: Macmillan Press, 1996), 103–41.
6. Chesterton, *Robert Louis Stevenson*, 171.
7. Frank McLynn, *Robert Louis Stevenson: A Biography* (London: Hutchinson, 1993), 235–6.
8. Robert Fraser, 'Nineteenth-century Adventure and Fantasy: James Morier, George Meredith, Lewis Carroll, and Robert Louis Stevenson' in Corinne Saunders (ed.), *A Companion to Romance from Classical to Contemporary* (Oxford: Blackwell Publishing, 2004), 389–405.
9. *'The Lantern-Bearers' and Other Essays*, ed. Jeremy Treglown (London: Chatto & Windus, 1988), 224–5. Mrs R. L. Stevenson, 'Note to *The Strange Case of Dr. Jekyll and Mr. Hyde*', IV, xix.
10. Sara Wasson, 'Olalla's Legacy: Twentieth-Century Vampire Fiction and Genetic Previvorship', *Journal of Stevenson Studies* 7 (2010), 55–81.
11. Hilary J. Beattie, 'Dreaming, Doubling and Gender in the Work of Robert Louis Stevenson: The Strange Case of "Olalla"', *Journal of Stevenson Studies* 2 (2005), 10–32.

12. William B. Jones, Jr (ed.), *Robert Louis Stevenson Reconsidered: New Critical Perspectives* (Jefferson, NC & London: McFarland, 2003), 3.
13. J. H. Millar, *A Literary History of Scotland* (London: T. Fisher Unwin, 1903), 651.
14. Arnold Kemp, 'Profit from Prejudice', *Observer* (Scottish edition), 21 April 2002.
15. Graham Balfour, *The Life of Robert Louis Stevenson*, 2 vols (London: Methuen, 1901), II, 13.
16. Jenni Calder, *R.L.S.: A Life Study* (London: Hamish Hamilton, 1980), 220.
17. McLynn, *Robert Louis Stevenson*, 254–5. Nellie Van De Grift Sanchez, *The Life of Mrs. Robert Louis Stevenson* (London: Chatto & Windus, 1920), 118.
18. Edwin M. Eigner, *Robert Louis Stevenson and Romantic Tradition* (Princeton: Princeton University Press, 1966), 143–64. Sandison, *Robert Louis Stevenson*, 215–69.
19. *Strange Case of Dr Jekyll and Mr Hyde*, ed. Roger Luckhurst (Oxford: Oxford University Press, 2006), 5.
20. Balfour, *The Life*, II, 13.
21. Wayne Koestenbaum, *Double Talk: The Erotics of Male Literary Collaboration* (New York & London: Routledge, 1989), 143–77. Elaine Showalter, *Sexual Anarchy: Gender and Culture at the Fin de Siècle* (London: Bloomsbury, 1990), 105–26.
22. Linda Dryden, *The Modern Gothic and Literary Doubles: Stevenson, Wilde and Wells* (Basingstoke: Palgrave Macmillan, 2003), 75.
23. Stephen Arata, *Fictions of Loss in the Victorian Fin de Siècle* (Cambridge: Cambridge University Press, 1996), 33–53.
24. Julia Reid, *Robert Louis Stevenson, Science, and the Fin de Siècle* (Basingstoke: Palgrave Macmillan, 2006), 55ff; 94.
25. Sara Clayson, ' "Steadfastly and securely on his upward path": Dr Jekyll's Spiritualist Experiment', *Journal of Stevenson Studies* 2 (2005), 51–69.
26. Thomas L. Reed, Jr, *The Transforming Draught: Jekyll and Hyde, Robert Louis Stevenson and the Victorian Alcohol Debate* (Jefferson NC & London: MacFarland, 2006).
27. Mark Currie, *Postmodern Narrative Theory* (London: Macmillan, 1998), 117–34.
28. *The Letters of Robert Louis Stevenson*, ed. Bradford A. Booth and Ernest Mehew, 8 vols (New Haven & London: Yale University Press, 1994–5), vol. 5, 336. This letter is not included in Mehew.
29. *Kidnapped*, ed. Ian Duncan (Oxford: Oxford University Press, 2014), 23. Subsequent references are to this edition.
30. Sandison, *Robert Louis Stevenson*, 193.
31. Sandison, *Robert Louis Stevenson*, 179.

32. David Daiches, *Robert Louis Stevenson* (Norfolk, Conn.: New Directions, 1947), 55.
33. Reid, *Robert Louis Stevenson*, 125.
34. *Robert Louis Stevenson's Kidnapped*: The Original Text, ed. Barry Menikoff (San Marino, Calif.: Huntington Library, 1999).
35. Barry Menikoff, *Narrating Scotland: The Imagination of Robert Louis Stevenson* (Columbia, SC: University of South Carolina Press, 2005), 206.

CHAPTER 4: 'VOICES IN THE DARKNESS'

1. Alan Sandison, *Robert Louis Stevenson and the Appearance of Modernism* (Basingstoke & London: Macmillan Press, 1996), 270–316. *The Master of Ballantrae*, ed. Adrian Poole (London: Penguin Books, 1996), vii–xxvi. Hereafter quoted as Poole.
2. David Daiches, *Robert Louis Stevenson* (Norfolk, Conn.: New Directions, 1947), 74–85.
3. Eric Massie, 'Scottish Gothic: Robert Louis Stevenson, *The Master of Ballantrae* and *The Private Memoirs and Confessions of a Justified Sinner*' in William B. Jones, Jr, *Robert Louis Stevenson Reconsidered: New Critical Perspectives* (Jefferson NC & London: McFarland, 2003), 163–73.
4. Hilary J. Beattie, ' "The interest of the attraction exercised by the great RLS of those days": Robert Louis Stevenson, Henry James and the Influence of Friendship', *Journal of Stevenson Studies* 4 (2007), 91–113.
5. Poole, 221–8.
6. D. H. Lawrence, *Studies in Classic American Literature*, ed. Ezra Greenspan, Lindeth Vasey, and John Worthen (Cambridge: Cambridge University Press, 2003), 14.
7. Poole, vii.
8. *The Letters of Robert Louis Stevenson*, ed. Bradford A. Booth and Edwin Mehew, 8 vols (New Haven & London: Yale University Press, 1994–5), vol. 6, 277.
9. Ann C. Colley, *Robert Louis Stevenson and the Colonial Imagination* (Aldershot: Ashgate, 2004).
10. Sylvie Largeaud-Ortega, 'Stevenson's "little tale" is a "library": an anthropological approach to "The Beach of Falesá" ', *Journal of Stevenson Studies* 6 (2008), 117–34.
11. *South Sea Tales*, ed. Roslyn Jolly (Oxford: Oxford University Press, 1996), 11. This edition is used for references from both 'The Beach of Falesá' and *The Ebb-Tide*.
12. Barry Menikoff, *Robert Louis Stevenson and 'The Beach of Falesá': A*

Study in Victorian Publishing (Edinburgh: Edinburgh University Press, 1984), 82–3.

13. *The Collected Poems of Robert Louis Stevenson,* ed. Robert C. Lewis in *The Collected Works of Robert Louis Stevenson* (Edinburgh: Edinburgh University Press, 2003), 196–7.

14. Claire Harman, *Robert Louis Stevenson: A Biography* (London: HarperCollins, 2005), 429.

15. Daiches, *Robert Louis Stevenson,* 99–140.

16. Frank McLynn, *Robert Louis Stevenson: A Biography* (London: Hutchinson, 1993), 492.

17. Edward J. Cowan, ' "Intent upon my own race and place I wrote": Robert Louis Stevenson and Scottish History', in *The Polar Twins,* ed. Edward J. Cowan and Douglas Gifford (Edinburgh: John Donald Publishers, 1999), 187–214, 191.

18. *Kidnapped* and *Catriona,* ed. Emma Letley (Oxford & New York: Oxford University Press, 1986), xix–xx. Roslyn Jolly, *Robert Louis Stevenson in the Pacific: Travel, Empire, and the Author's Profession* (Farnham: Ashgate, 2009).

CHAPTER 5: 'UNDER THE WIDE AND STARRY SKY'

1. James Robertson, 'A Reliable Author and his Unreliable Critics: The Fall and Rise of Stevenson's Literary Reputation', *Journal of Stevenson Studies* 8 (2011), 5–16.

2. Hilary J. Beattie, 'Stormy Nights and Headless Women: Heterosexual Conflict and Desire in the Work of Robert Louis Stevenson', *Journal of Stevenson Studies* 6 (2009), 63–80.

3. Roderick Watson, ' "Ginger beer and earthquakes" – Stevenson and the Terrors of Contingency', *Journal of Stevenson Studies* 8 (2011), 108–24.

4. Rosalind Williams, *The Triumph of Human Empire: Verne, Morris, and Stevenson at the End of the World* (Chicago & London: University of Chicago Press, 2013).

5. Harold Bloom (ed.), *Bloom's Modern Critical Views: Robert Louis Stevenson* (Philadelphia: Chelsea House, 2005), 2.

6. Barry Menikoff, *Narrating Scotland: The Imagination of Robert Louis Stevenson* (Columbia, SC: University of South Carolina Press, 2005), 203.

Select Bibliography

In the decades after Stevenson's death, a large number of complete editions of his writings appeared on both sides of the Atlantic, though some were essentially reprints of earlier versions. Most large libraries are likely to have one or other of these in their catalogue. No new complete edition has been published, however, since the 1920s. Edinburgh University Press began to issue a modern scholarly edition in 1995. This stalled in 2004 but has been revived and is currently under way once more. In the preparation of this book, however, it was the Skerryvore Edition from 1924, with notes by Lloyd Osbourne and Fanny Stevenson, which was at hand.

Equally, the number of editions of individual works published since his death is immense and ever-growing. As a rule, readers of the present book are best directed to the popular scholarly editions in two series: Oxford World Classics and Penguin Classics. These series offer generally excellent modern editions of some of Stevenson's most famous stories, but particular works are not invariably to be found in the two catalogues and fresh editions are periodically substituted for somewhat older ones, making it difficult to refer readers simply to a particular editor's version. Furthermore, in all but one case (*The Master of Ballantrae*, ed. Adrian Poole (London: Penguin Books, 1996)), Stevenson's titles in Penguin Classics are now available from the publisher solely as electronic texts. At the time of writing, there are only four Stevenson titles in World Classics. These have been used with the Penguin *Master of Ballantrae* in the endnotes to this book, and are listed here.

Kidnapped, ed. Ian Duncan (Oxford: Oxford University Press, 2014)
South Sea Tales, ed. Roslyn Jolly [for 'The Beach of Falesá' and *The Ebb-Tide*] (Oxford: Oxford University Press, 1996)

Strange Case of Dr Jekyll and Mr Hyde and Other Tales, ed. Roger Luckhurst
    (Oxford: Oxford University Press, 2006)
Treasure Island, ed. Peter Hunt (Oxford: Oxford University Press, 2011)

WORKS

The order in which works are discussed in the text follows the date of
writing. The following list gives, however, the date of first British book
publication.

Travels with a Donkey in the Cevennes (London: Kegan Paul, 1879)
New Arabian Nights (London: Chatto & Windus, 1882)
Treasure Island (London: Cassell, 1883)
Prince Otto: A Romance (London: Chatto & Windus, 1885)
More New Arabian Nights: The Dynamiter (London: Longmans, Green,
    1885)
Strange Case of Dr Jekyll and Mr Hyde (London: Longmans, Green, 1886)
Kidnapped (London: Cassell, 1886)
'The Merry Men' and Other Tales and Fables (London: Chatto & Windus,
    1887) [includes 'The Merry Men', 'Thrawn Janet', 'Markheim',
    'Olalla', 'The Treasure of Franchard']
The Black Arrow (London: Cassell, 1888)
The Master of Ballantrae (London: Cassell, 1889)
Island Nights' Entertainments (London: Cassell, 1893) [contains 'The
    Beach of Falesá', 'The Bottle Imp', and 'The Isle of Voices']
Catriona (London: Cassell, 1893)
The Ebb-Tide (London: Heinemann, 1894)
'The Misadventures of John Nicholson', *The Works of Robert Louis
    Stevenson* ['The Edinburgh Edition'], vol. 22 (London: Chatto &
    Windus, 1894–8). [This was the first British printing of the story in
    book form. 'The Edinburgh Edition' was the first of many collected
    editions of Stevenson's works. However, the first publication in
    book form to appear anywhere had been an American pirated
    edition (New York: George Munro, 1887). The subtitle 'A Chrismas
    Story' had been added by the publisher when the story first
    appeared in Cassell's Christmas annual *Yule Tide* in 1887.]
Weir of Hermiston (London: Chatto & Windus, 1896)

BIOGRAPHIES AND LETTERS

Balfour, Graham, *The Life of Robert Louis Stevenson*, 2 vols (London:
    Methuen, 1901)

Bell, Ian, *Robert Louis Stevenson: A Biography* (Edinburgh: Mainstream, 1992)

Booth, Bradford A. and Mehew, Ernest (eds), *The Letters of Robert Louis Stevenson*, 8 vols (New Haven & London: Yale University Press, 1994–5)

Calder, Jenni, *R. L. S.: A Life Study* (London: Hamish Hamilton, 1980)

Callow, Philip, *Louis: A Life of Robert Louis Stevenson* (London: Constable, 2001)

Daiches, David, *Robert Louis Stevenson and his World* (London: Thames & Hudson, 1973)

Furnas, J. C., *Voyage to Windward: The Life of Robert Louis Stevenson* (London: Faber & Faber, 1952)

Gray, William, *Robert Louis Stevenson: A Literary Life* (Basingstoke: Palgrave Macmillan, 2004)

Harman, Claire, *Robert Louis Stevenson: A Biography* (London: Harper-Collins, 2005)

Mehew, Ernest (ed.), *Selected Letters of Robert Louis Stevenson* (New Haven & London: Yale University Press, 2001)

McLynn, Frank, *Robert Louis Stevenson: A Biography* (London: Hutchinson, 1993)

Sanchez, Nellie Van De Grift, *The Life of Mrs. Robert Louis Stevenson* (London: Chatto & Windus, 1920)

CRITICAL STUDIES

Arata, Stephen, *Fictions of Loss in the Victorian Fin de Siècle* (Cambridge: Cambridge University Press, 1996)

Beattie, Hilary J., 'Dreaming, Doubling and Gender in the Work of Robert Louis Stevenson: The Strange Case of "Olalla"', *Journal of Stevenson Studies* 2 (2005), 10–32

————, '"The interest of the attraction exercised by the great RLS of those days": Robert Louis Stevenson, Henry James and the Influence of Friendship', *Journal of Stevenson Studies* 4 (2007), 91–113

————, 'Stormy Nights and Headless Women: Heterosexual Conflict and Desire in the Work of Robert Louis Stevenson', *Journal of Stevenson Studies* 6 (2009), 63–80

Bloom, Harold (ed.), *Bloom's Modern Critical Views: Robert Louis Stevenson* (Philadelphia: Chelsea House, 2005)

Bristow, Joseph, *Empire Boys: Adventures in a Man's World* (London: HarperCollins Academic, 1991)

Buckton, Oliver S., '"Faithful to his map": Profit and Desire in Robert Louis Stevenson's *Treasure Island*', *Journal of Stevenson Studies* 1 (2004), 138–49

Chesterton, G. K., *Robert Louis Stevenson* (London: Hodder & Stoughton, 1927)

Clayson, Sara, '"Steadfastly and securely on his upward path": Dr Jekyll's Spiritualist Experiment', *Journal of Stevenson Studies* 2 (2005), 51–69

Colley, Ann C., *Robert Louis Stevenson and the Colonial Imagination* (Aldershot: Ashgate, 2004)

Cowan, Edward J., '"Intent Upon My Own Race and Place I Wrote": Robert Louis Stevenson and Scottish History', in Edward J. Cowan and Douglas Gifford (eds), *The Polar Twins* (Edinburgh: John Donald Publishers, 1999)

Crawford, Robert, *Scotland's Books: The Penguin History of Scottish Literature* (London: Penguin Books, 2007)

Currie, Mark, *Postmodern Narrative Theory* (London: Macmillan, 1998)

Daiches, David, *Robert Louis Stevenson* (Norfolk, Conn.: New Directions, 1947)

Dryden, Linda, *The Modern Gothic and Literary Doubles: Stevenson, Wilde and Wells* (Basingstoke: Palgrave Macmillan, 2003)

———, Stephen Arata, Eric Massie (eds), *Robert Louis Stevenson and Joseph Conrad: Writers of Transition* (Lubbock: Texas Tech University Press, 2009)

Eigner, Edwin M., *Robert Louis Stevenson and Romantic Tradition* (Princeton: Princeton University Press, 1966)

Fielding, Penny, 'Robert Louis Stevenson' in Susan Manning (ed.), *Enlightenment, Britain and Empire (1707–1918), The Edinburgh History of Scottish Literature*, vol. 2 (Edinburgh: Edinburgh University Press, 2007), 324–30

Fowler, Alistair, 'Parables of Adventure: The Debatable Novels of Robert Louis Stevenson', in Ian Campbell (ed.) *Nineteenth-Century Scottish Fiction: Critical Essays*, (Manchester: Carcanet New Press, 1979), 105–29

Fraser, Robert, *Victorian Quest Romance: Stevenson, Haggard, Kipling and Conan Doyle* (Plymouth: Northcote House, 1998)

Hammond, J. R., *A Robert Louis Stevenson Companion* (London & Basingstoke: Macmillan, 1984)

Hart, Francis R., 'Robert Louis Stevenson in Prose' in Douglas Gifford (ed.), *The History of Scottish Literature,* volume 3, 'Nineteenth Century' (Aberdeen: Aberdeen University Press, 1988), 291–308

Jolly, Roslyn, *Robert Louis Stevenson in the Pacific: Travel, Empire, and the Author's Profession* (Farnham: Ashgate, 2009)

Jones, William B. Jr., *Robert Louis Stevenson Reconsidered: New Critical Perspectives* (Jefferson NC & London: McFarland, 2003)

Kiely, Robert, *Robert Louis Stevenson and the Fiction of Adventure* (Cambridge, Mass.: Harvard University Press, 1965)

Koestenbaum, Wayne, *Double Talk: The Erotics of Male Literary Collabora-tion* (New York & London: Routledge, 1989)

Largeaud-Ortega, Sylvie, 'Stevenson's "little tale" is a "library": an anthropological approach to "The Beach of Falesá"', *Journal of Stevenson Studies* 6 (2008), 117–34

Maixner, Paul, *Robert Louis Stevenson: The Critical Heritage* (London, Boston, & Henley: Routledge & Kegan Paul, 1981)

Menikoff, Barry, *Narrating Scotland: The Imagination of Robert Louis Stevenson* (Columbia, S.C.: University of South Carolina Press, 2005)

—— (ed.), *Robert Louis Stevenson's Kidnapped: The Original Text* (San Marino, Calif.: Huntington Library, 1999)

Millar, J. H., *A Literary History of Scotland* (London: T. Fisher Unwin, 1903)

Norquay, Glenda, *Robert Louis Stevenson and Theories of Reading* (Manchester & New York: Manchester University Press, 2007)

Reed, Thomas L. Jr., *The Transforming Draught: Jekyll and Hyde, Robert Louis Stevenson and the Victorian Alcohol Debate* (Jefferson NC & London: MacFarland, 2006)

Reid, Julia, *Robert Louis Stevenson, Science, and the Fin de Siècle* (Basingstoke: Palgrave Macmillan, 2006)

Riach, Alan, *Representing Scotland in Literature, Popular Culture and Iconography* (Basingstoke: Palgrave Macmillan, 2005)

Robertson, James, 'A Reliable Author and his Unreliable Critics: The Fall and Rise of Stevenson's Literary Reputation', *Journal of Stevenson Studies* 8 (2011), 5–16

Sandison, Alan, *Robert Louis Stevenson and the Appearance of Modernism* (Basingstoke & London: Macmillan Press, 1996)

Saunders, Corinne (ed.), *A Companion to Romance from Classical to Contemporary* (Oxford: Blackwell Publishing, 2004)

Showalter, Elaine, *Sexual Anarchy: Gender and Culture at the Fin de Siècle* (London: Bloomsbury, 1990)

Treglown Jeremy (ed.), *Robert Louis Stevenson 'The Lantern-Bearers' and Other Essays* (London: Chatto & Windus, 1988)

Wasson, Sara, 'Olalla's Legacy: Twentieth-Century Vampire Fiction and Genetic Previvorship', *Journal of Stevenson Studies* 7 (2010), 55–81

Watson, Roderick, ' "Ginger beer and earthquakes" – Stevenson and the Terrors of Contingency', *Journal of Stevenson Studies* 8 (2011), 108–24

Williams, Rosalind, *The Triumph of Human Empire: Verne, Morris, and Stevenson at the End of the World* (Chicago & London: University of Chicago Press, 2013)

Index

Printed and bound by CPI Group (UK) Ltd, Croydon, CR0 4YY

13/04/2025

14656594-0003